GETTING BENT

The Perfect Bend

Perfecting Golf Club Hosel Adjustments

Jeff Sheets

Design, Photography, Illustrations and Editing by Jeff Sheets

© 2008 By Jeffrey D. Sheets

First Printing – January 2009

ISBN: 0-615-26956-7
ISBN 978-0-615-26956-6

www.jeffsheetsgolf.com

All rights reserved.
No portion of this publication may be reproduced or transmitted in any form or by any means, electronic or mechanical, including photography, recording, or any information storage and retrieval system, without permission in writing from the publisher, except by a reviewer who may quote brief passages in critical article or review to be printed in a magazine, newspaper, or electronically transmitted on radio or television.

Printed in the United States of America

Sheets Publishing
Round Rock, Texas, U.S.A.
www.sheetspublishing.com

Table of Contents

Overview of Iron Adjustments   1
The equipment necessary to get the job done

Bending Forged Irons   4
Working with carbon steel

Bending Investment Cast Irons   6
An overview of cast stainless steels
Home shop heat treating   7

Adjusting Irons – Cause & Effect   15

Iron Loft Adjustments
    Objectives   16
    The Execution   18

Iron Lie Adjustments
    Objectives   19
    The Execution   22

Iron Loft & Lie Compound Bends
    The Execution   22

Overview of Wood Loft & Lie Adjustments   25

Wood Lie Adjustments – Objectives   29

Wood Loft & Face Angle Adjustments
    Cause & Effect   31

Table of Contents

Wood Lie Angle Adjustments
    The Execution   35

Wood Loft & Face Angle Adjustments
    The Execution   35

Overview of Putter Loft & Lie Adjustments   39

Bending Different Putter Materials   44

Putter Loft & Lie Adjustments
    Cause & Effect   46
    The Execution   51

Introduction

      I recall my nervousness with the first set of irons that I adjusted the loft and lies on. Without having experienced the feedback of resistance-and-give of a hosel I wasn't sure what to expect with that first club. Fortunately it was a forged iron which accepted a bend very smoothly. I was able to adjust the remainder of the set with the same amount of ease. However it wasn't long before I found myself bending the hosels of a set of 17-4 stainless steel castings. The task turned into a completely different result. While successful, the manner in which each hosel bent, the amount of adjustment each head would accept, and the ability to hit the loft and lie specs appeared to be random acts in futility. How could the same chore have completely different results between these two types of sets? My indoctrination into hosel bending was to continue on for the next ten years as the golf industry transitioned from predominantly soft forged irons to investment cast 6-4 titanium alloys.

      There are a multitude of different materials used in the manufacturing of golf club heads these days. The majority of irons and woods are either investment cast or undergo some form of forged stamping. Each manufacturing process in addition to the material type results in a golf club that has its own personality regarding hosel adjustments. Add into the mix a variety of putter materials and manufacturing processes and you've got yourself a potpourri of bending variables.

      Today I have no fear in adjusting any golf club head. There is a proper approach to take with each combination of head material and the process in which is was produced. I have written *The Perfect Bend* to guide both the novice and experienced golf club technician in the art of hosel bending. Knowing how to bend is only half of the job. Understanding the cause and effect on the golf club's specs is the other half. Within these pages I will show you how to be successful in the pursuit of each. Enjoy the act of getting bent.

                                        Jeff Sheets

Getting Bent

Everything you ever wanted to know about hosel adjustments but were afraid to ask . . .

Loft & Lie Adjustments

While grip replacements are the bread and butter for many golf club technicians iron hosel adjustments for lofts and lies follows behind as a close second. Anyone can re-grip clubs because no special tools are required. When it comes to loft and lie adjustments there is a need for a special fixture to hold the clubhead commonly referred to as a *loft/lie machine.* Technically the device is more of a vice; not a machine, since it doesn't run on a motor or engine.

Whether you are adjusting irons, woods or putters it is important to have a device that can tightly hold the clubhead in place because a good amount of force will be placed on the hosel to alter its position in relation to the face and sole.

Loft & Lie Adjustments for Irons

Since the majority of loft/lie machines sold are for irons it goes without saying that they are the most commonly adjusted of the different clubhead types. There are two necessary pieces of equipment required to adjust an iron's loft/lie angles. First there is the loft/lie machine which holds the clubhead in a secured position. The second item required is a bending bar which will have a knuckle at one end which wraps around the iron's hosel. The bar is leveraged in the appropriate direction to execute the adjustment. Not all loft/lie machines are sold with the bending bar so you may have to purchase the two items independently.

All models will need to be mounted to a stationary floor stand, work bench or counter. There are some floor stands that do not need to be permanently mounted because they are designed with a platform that the technician stands on to keep the unit from moving during the hosel bend. I personally prefer working with a bending unit that is securely anchored to the floor or counter surface. Standing on a platform to keep the iron in place can be distracting as you are executing a bend.

Loft/lie machines can vary quite greatly in price. The most basic units hold the clubhead in a fixed position so that it will not move as the hosel is being adjusted. These basic units do not have any type of measurement gauges on them to provide you with the loft or lie angle specifications. Instead you must first measure the club's loft and lie specification on another device (such as a clubhead auditing unit) then proceed by placing the iron in the loft/lie machine to execute the bend. Once the adjustment is made the iron is re-measured on the auditing unit with hopefully the correct specification you are shooting for. If not, it's back into the loft/lie machine for another bend and back to the auditing unit for measurement again.

Usually a novice technician will opt to purchase the least expensive loft/lie machine but it is also the novice that requires the greatest number of adjustments to hit the specification target. A great deal of time can be spent transitioning back and forth between the loft/lie machine and the auditing unit. This is why I recommend at least a mid-priced loft/lie machine from the start. Not only are you purchasing the unit to hold the head securely but also the gauges necessary to read the head specifications.

The majority of loft/lie machines sold incorporate some form of measuring gauge. Construction may consist of 100% machined steel or aluminum, or a variety of metals and plastic parts. The materials and construction influence the loft/lie machine's selling price. The higher end models will be 100% machined for both accuracy and durability.

When I first began working on the PGA Tour in the late 1980's I used an old loft/lie machine called the Van-L. It had a highly inaccurate measurement scale and only a so-so head clamp which did not do a good job at keeping the head immobile during the hosel adjustment. Using the Van-L was akin to using a screw driver to pound a nail in place. While it was possible to get the job done it pales in comparison to the efficiency and accuracy of today's loft/lie machines.

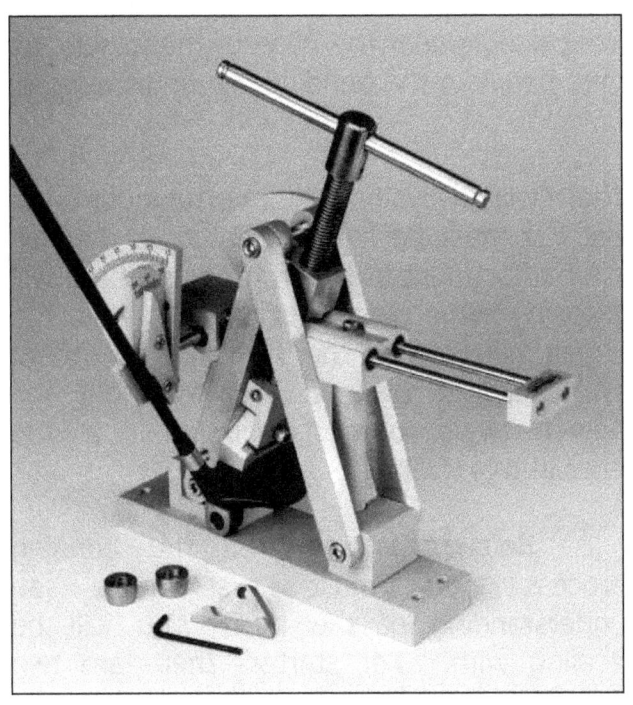

I was the first club technician to use the Ed Mitchell Steel Club® loft/lie machine out on the PGA Tour. The unit was great because I could execute my adjustments and accurately read the specs without ever removing the iron from the unit. The Steel Club continues to be the Cadillac of loft/lie machines today however there is an equally excellent unit at a fraction of the price in the Golfsmith Ultimate Loft/Lie Bending Unit. It is quicker to use when jumping between right and left handed adjustments and much kinder to the top lines (it won't crush them) on many of today's thin iron designs. In addition the Ultimate unit can also measure and adjust hybrid hosels.

While the design and construction of the loft/lie machine can be important the style of the bending bar can be of equal significance to the club technician. There have been bending bars of various lengths, weight and knuckle design over the years. Many technicians prefer using a knuckle constructed of brass because it leaves the fewest marks on the iron's hosel. While brass may be gentle with chrome plated forgings it may not have the long term durability to deal with years (or months) of 17-4 stainless steel adjustments. For this reason I prefer a bar with a hardened steel knuckle for durability purposes.

Bending bars come in a variety of designs. Find one or multiple models that you feel comfortable working with.

Some knuckles are fixed in their size and others are adjustable. Adjustable knuckles are intended to provide a tight clamp onto the hosel regardless of the hosel's diameter. Keep in mind that a bending bar with moving parts can lead to its own wear and failure sooner than one without adjust ability. The knuckle designs you will find in most high volume operations, or even the foundries producing the heads, are a fixed size.

The Perfect Bend

A bending bar with a chamfered or counter-sunk knuckle opening is versatile. I have found these to work well on even the shortest of hosel lengths. The chamfer permits the knuckle to seat deeply near the base of the hosel. Its counter-sunk design relives stress points between the bending bar and the hosel for minimizing dings to the hosel.

When executing a hosel bend there will always be the opportunity to dent, crease, pinch or even break the hosel. It must be communicated to the golf club's owner that even with a successful adjustment of the iron hosels there will likely be some blemishes resulting from the stress caused by the bending operation. We'll get into some of these situations and how to avoid some of their pitfalls a little later in this book.

This bending bar knuckle has two bevelled openings to allow a snug grasp at the bottom of the hosel.

Before jumping into the bending process you must first have an understanding of the metal you will be dealing with. For starters there are two primary manufacturing methods for producing irons – forged and investment cast. Based on the manufacturing method you will have to manipulate the material that the iron is constructed from. This can have a great influence on whether the hosel adjustment happens easily or will require some elbow grease. Secondly, it influences how successful the adjustment can be made. Let's talk about the manufacturing methods and the associated types of steel you will be dealing with.

Bending Forged Hosels

Forged irons are constructed from a billet of carbon steel. The carbon steel has a high ductility rating to it which means is has elastic properties to the metal. In layman's terms the carbon steel bends easily. Experienced club technicians often state that forgings "bend like butter." Compared to the harder stainless steels the forged carbon steel feels butter-soft in its bend. Irons forged from carbon steel can be bent up to 4° without a great deal of force (Thrust Rating: 3-5). While this sounds like a winner to any club technician there is an important factor to keep in mind – chrome plating. The substrate of the carbon steel easily accepts an adjustment but the outer chrome plating that keeps the carbon steel from rusting will often begin to crinkle following 3° of bend. Therefore if you're adjusting a forged iron to 5° upright you will likely end up with an ugly crease or wrinkle of chrome plating on the hosel in the area of the bend.

The worst case scenario here is if the chrome plating crinkles enough to begin cracking and ultimately peeling off the hosel area. If you are bending an iron for someone else you must first discuss the potential of scaring the chrome plated surface as a result of the adjustment. I have seen some chrome plated hosel bends up to 7° before mischievous crinkling begins. However there are those cases where a 2° adjustment has led to chrome cracking. It is the chrome plating process, not the club technician or carbon steel that leads to the varied results on the hosel.

Protection to the hosel can be used by wrapping material around its circumference so that it is sandwiched between the hosel and bending bar knuckle. Leather is one material I've used with moderate success. It is good for preventing surface scratches caused by friction with the bending bar knuckle however it will not prevent the chrome from cracking or wrinkling if the hosel is bent too far.

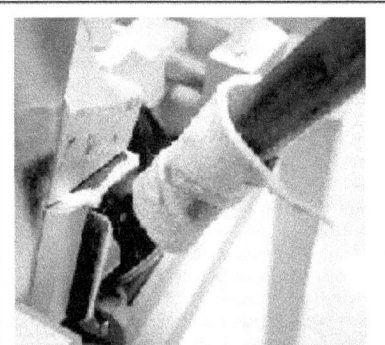

Wrapping leather around the hosel can help protect its surface from bending bar scratches.

Another material that works similarly is lead tape. Wrapping lead tape around the hosel provides a similar cushion as the leather. It's a good alternative if you are having difficulty keeping the leather in place however this method can become expensive over time as you use up your lead tape supply.

Thin sheets of brass can also be used. The same thin brass that many club technicians use for shimming shafts can be cut into pieces that are then wrapped around the hosel for protection. The thickness of the brass should be barely thin enough to cut with heavy duty scissors. Anything thicker will be difficult to work with.

To execute the adjustment to a forged iron a steady constant force should be used. Begin with a light level of force on the bending bar and gradually increase the pressure. As the soft carbon steel begins accepting the bend you will feel it give way to the force you are placing on it. This is what I call a *gradual pressure* bend to the hosel. The gradual pressure bend is best for softer steels which give into the bending force easier.

There are the odd irons that are forged from either hard or soft stainless steel billets. While these are less common materials used for forging you will find different reactions from these two different steels. In both cases there is no need to worry about chrome plating since the clubs are forged from stainless steel (they won't rust).

In recent years 410 stainless steel has been used for some forgings. It will bend easily (Thrust Rating: 3-5). You can likely achieve upwards of an 8° hosel adjustment on these irons without ill effects to the head's durability or cosmetics. Some wrinkling may take place at the point of bending stress but it can also easily be polished out for a smooth cosmetic look. As with the traditional forged carbon steel a gradual pressure should be used to bend the hosel.

It has been years since I have run across a forged 17-4 stainless steel head. Because the metal is so hard it takes a tremendous amount of force to forge a club head's shape. Subsequently it is very tough on the tooling (the forging dies). The ability to adjust the hosels of the forged 17-4 stainless steel heads will be similar to the adjust ability of investment cast 17-4 stainless steel parts. Two degrees is the recommended maximum for a 17-4 casting however you should be able to get an additional degree out of the forging. In this case use the *jerk* method to apply the adjustment force with the bending bar. When using the jerk method there is an immediate thrust of energy applied to the bend. This method is applicable to harder steels that are more resistant to accepting a hosel adjustment.

Both golfers and equipment technicians can be fooled by the term 'form forged.' A form forged iron is actually an investment cast iron that has undergone a stamping operation after is has been cast. The raw casting is placed in a form that squeezes the part under pressure making its molecular compaction tighter. This can be done with both stainless and carbon steel heads. Therefore particularly close attention should be paid to the type of material the iron was cast from. Follow the same guidelines for bending the appropriate material under the investment cast instructions.

Bending Investment Cast Irons

There are three primary materials used in premium investment cast iron heads today. They include the very hard 17-4 stainless steel, a moderately hard 431 stainless steel and a relatively soft 304 stainless steel. Inexpensive irons can also be die cast out of zinc and aluminum however neither of these two materials are suggested for bending. In a more specialized manner 8620 carbon steel is also used for investment casting wedges and putters. Stainless steel heads do not require any chrome plating so there is no concern over wrinkling or cracking a protective coating. However in the case of the 8620 carbon steel chrome plating is necessary to protect it from rusting. Let's work down the list of materials and their conduciveness to adjust ability.

17-4 Stainless Steel

For starters we must deal with 17-4 stainless steel. I use the word 'deal' because that's pretty much the situation with 17-4. You need to put up with its tough material characteristics which aren't necessary for most iron designs. 17-4 stainless steel was the most commonly used material in the earlier days of investment casting of irons. As recently as 20 years ago nearly all investment cast irons were cast in 17-4 stainless steel. Fortunately that is not the case today, however the odds that you will find yourself adjusting a 17-4 hosel are highly likely.

The ductility of 17-4 stainless steel will make the hosel very resistant to bending. In order to make a successful adjustment the 17-4 material requires heat treatment as previously discussed. With proper heat treatment the 17-4 hosel is capable of being bent 2° without any issues. The Thrust Rating resistance of the material will be in the 7-9 range. Using the jerk method to adjust the hosel is recommended. An initially strong force on the bending bar is the most successful technique in achieving a full 2° adjustment.

On occasion you may find yourself trying to make a hosel adjustment to a 17-4 head that was not heat treated. This is typical of lower quality head designs where the cost of the heat treatment is not desired by the manufacturer. A 17-4 iron that has not been heat treated will not want to accept a hosel adjustment. As you apply the force on the bending bar you will feel a resistance to any movement. When trying to adjust a non-heat treated head you will likely snap the hosel off before you will successfully adjust it. When you run across a set of non-heat treated irons it is best to avoid adjusting them. Heart ache will likely follow if you choose to take on the task – unless you elect to do some heat treating yourself.

Heat treating anneals the club's metal so that it can be adjusted. While it is executed using industrial equipment you will find that you can achieve similar results at home. You will have to begin with the set of irons un-shafted. Spread the heads across a baking rack allowing maximum air circulation around each part. Place the heads into an over at 350°F for two hours. Allow the heads to gradually cool on the wire rack so air can circulate around each head cooling down. The final product might not smell like an inviting batch of chocolate chip cookies but the steel is now kind enough to accept up to a 2° bend.

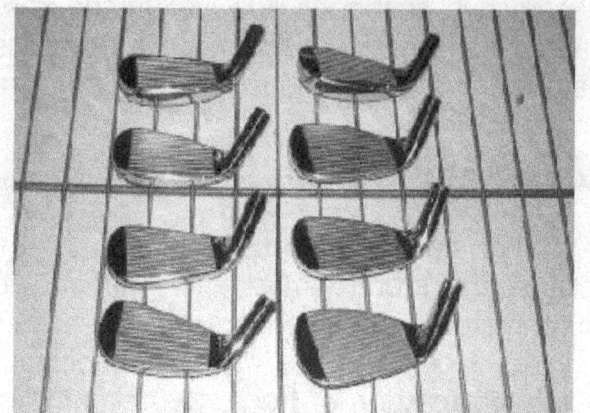

Home made heat treatment method - Heat oven to 350°F. Place 17-4 stainless steel heads on the center rack separated apart so they do not touch one another. Heat for 2 hours. Allow to air cool enabling heads to cool down at an even rate.

There have been occasions where I was required to bend a set of irons upwards of 4°-10°. My first few attempts at it were with Ping Eye2 irons. It was easy enough to get a couple of degrees bend out of them but I had to develop my hot hosel method to bend well past 2°. To begin with the shafts need to be pulled from the 17-4 stainless steel heads.

The head to be adjusted is secured into the loft/lie machine. I will use either a solid steel rod or a steel shaft placed in the hosel so I can read the loft and lie before making the adjustment. The hosel must be heated red hot using a propane torch in order to bend it so the shaft must be removed from the hosel as it is heated cherry red. Once the entire hosel is red hot place the shaft back into it and secure the bending bar over the hosel. At this point the hosel will bend very easily. Thrust Rating: 1-3 using a gradual pressure bend. It is important to have the steel shaft or rod in the hosel as the adjustment is taking place. The hosel is very soft when it has been heated to a red glow and it can easily be crushed by the bending bar if it does not have any internal support.

Adjust the hosel to the desired loft and lie specification and then remove the shaft. With leather gloves on for protection, carefully remove the iron from the loft/lie machine and quench it in a bucket of cold water (which I always have standing by for such jobs). Once the iron has cooled, place it back into the loft/lie machine for measurement. If the specs are within 2° of the desired target the hosel can be cold bent at this time to the final loft and lie. However if one of the specs is more than 2° off it is recommended to reheat the hosel with propane and execute the hot hosel adjustment procedure one more time.

Following this operation the hosel will be discolored from the intense heat. You will need to match the finish of the hosel to the rest of the head using the appropriate surface finishing techniques. Satin and mirror finishes are the most common used on irons today.

Regardless whether heat is applied to the hosel for bending it, a home based heat treatment is done or the iron hosels are cold bent, 17-4 stainless steel has a natural tendency to want to spring back to its original cast position. This is the result of metal memory.

My first experience with 17-4 stainless steel memory was shortly after I accepted my first PGA Tour club technician job. Working in the tour van I ran through numerous loft and lie adjustments on a daily basis. The majority of irons I saw were carbon steel forgings and the few players using 17-4 castings were Ping staff members. I had adjusted numerous sets of Ping Eye2s before running across my first encounter with specification 'bounce back' as I called it.

I had just completed a set of loft and lie adjustments to a player's set of Ping Eye2s when he returned to the equipment trailer less than 10 minutes later stating that the lie angles appeared to have popped back to their original position. I had adjusted the set 2° upright and promptly measured the set I had worked on only minutes earlier. He was right – many of the lie angles were back at their original spec prior to my bending them. I made the adjustments one more time and asked the player to hit a few balls with each, then I would measure them once again.

And again a number of the lie angles bounced back to their original spec. The shock of the impact of the balls was kicking the hosel angle to its original cast position.

To combat the bounce back problem for a third time I bent the first club 3° upright. With the iron still locked into the loft/lie machine I grabbed the grip end of the club and placed a strong load (bend) on the shaft. I then let it go, allowing it to spring quickly while hitting the hosel with a ball peen hammer at the same time. A couple of good hits with the hammer and I knew if the hosel was going to bounce back it would do it then.

Upon measuring the lie it had bounced back 1.5°. Since I had bent it 3° upright I was now only ½° from my final target. I adjusted the hosel another

Clockwise from below: Materials required for a hot bend - propane torch, hosel rod (or steel shaft), gloves, water bucket. bending bar and safety equipment.

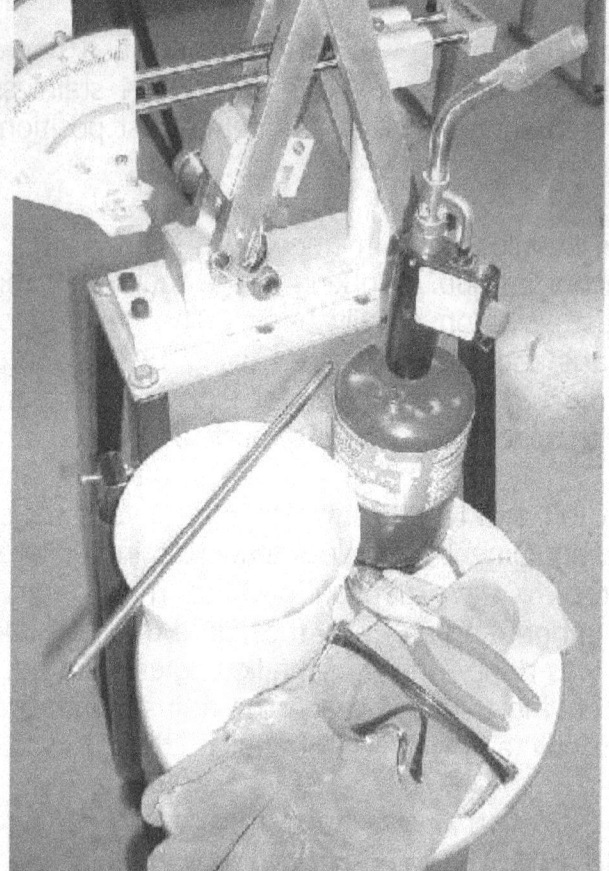

Heat hosel with the propane torch until it is red hot. Install rod into it before bending.

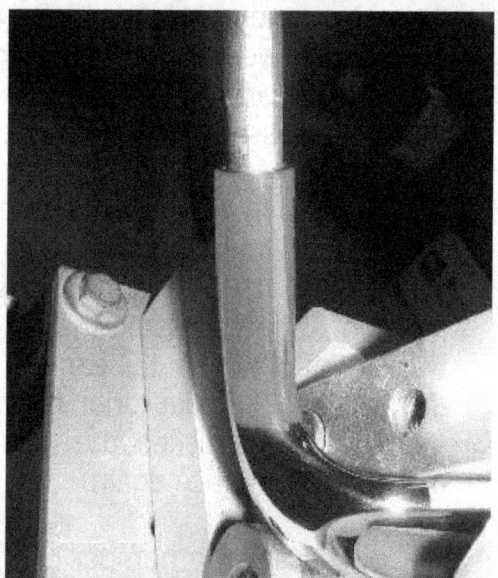

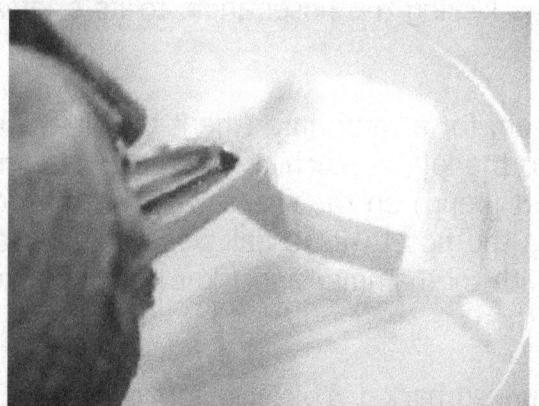

Carefully remove head from the bending machine with gloves (and pliers if necessary). Quench in a bucket of cold water. Re-measure. Cold adjust if within 2°, otherwise re-heat hosel for a greater bend.

Execute the bend. Limit the bend to less than 10°. Measure and readjust as necessary.

full degree upright, sprang the shaft and hit the hosel with the hammer. The hosel only bounced back ½° settling in on the final spec of 2° upright.

Before continuing adjusting the rest of the set I had the tour pro hit some shots on the range with the club and immediately re-measured the specs. Fortunately there was no change.

I proceeded to adjust the remainder of the set one last time. Most of the irons required a hosel bend that was 1°-2° beyond the desired spec. With each club I sprang the shaft (which imparts a great deal of vibration to the hosel) and hit the hosel with the ball peen hammer. This protocol overcame the natural metal memory of the 17-4 stainless steel by shocking it back to the desired specification.

For the next dozen cast 17-4 steel iron sets I bent I paid particularly close attention to the metal memory. In many cases there was no need to bend beyond the target spec. However in 100% of the cases I sprang the shaft and shocked the hosel with the hammer. In fact this became so much a part of my bending routine that a ball peen hammer hung alongside the bending bar by my loft/lie machine.

When adjusting 17-4 stainless steel hosels it is important to ensure that clubs you have bent are not going to spring back after being hit. Take a cue from an old time tour technician that getting a job done right is making sure you're not going to see that set again (unless it's for some other type of work).

431 Stainless Steel

While it has been available for many decades 431 stainless steel took awhile to catch on as the material of choice for irons with golf club manufacturers. I have been a fan of it dating back many years. Compared to 17-4 stainless steel 431 has more ductility to its properties. This allows a greater degree of hosel bend ability. In nearly all cases you should get a 2° hosel adjustment using moderate-to-high pressure. For an experienced club technician a 4° adjustment is achievable.

To bend a 431 stainless steel hosel the jerk method is recommended. However some club technicians prefer the gradual pressure method using a greater deal of force than used with forged carbon steel. The greatest beauty of the 431 material is that it has no metal memory. Once you make an adjustment to the hosel it will remain in its new position. This is a great advantage over 17-4 stainless steel which wants to spring back to its original cast specification.

As with the 17-4 steel you can heat the hosel red hot using a propane torch to pursue a much greater bend upwards of 10°.

There is an iteration of 431 stainless steel that incorporates a higher amount of nickel in its material content. Known by a variety of different names I have most commonly found this material to be called either 431-1 or 431-TTL stainless steel. This material undergoes an additional heat treatment process to increase the metal's ductility so additional elongation can occur. Simply put these versions of the 431 stainless steel can be adjusted upwards of 10°-13° degrees without the assistance of heating up the hosel (basically a cold bend). As with traditional 431 stainless steel both the jerk and gradual pressure methods work well depending on the technician making the adjustments.

304 Stainless Steel

304 stainless steel is most commonly used in traditional size irons and wedges. Its material properties are not strong enough to support the thinner face construction of oversize irons. One positive characteristic of its material properties is very high ductility. Irons produced from 304 stainless steel can easily be adjusted up and often beyond 10°. Use the gradual pressure bending method. You'll find that the material provides a similar feel to forged carbon steel. It would since both have similar material properties to them. The Thrust Rating of 304 stainless steel is 3-6.

As with the 431 stainless steel the 304 stainless has no metal memory to it. Once you have made the adjustment it will remain in that position. Due to the material's soft metal characteristics the loft and lies of the iron should be checked regularly. This is particularly true when the golfer using them has an aggressive downward angle of attack and also if playing on firm turf conditions. Both of these elements place ample force on the iron's sole to alter its hosel setting over time.

8620 Carbon Steel

You will find the 8620 carbon steel to be very similar to the forged carbon steel and the cast 304 stainless steel when it comes to making hosel adjustments. All three of these materials have a similar Rockwell hardness (HRB85-90). The feel of the 8620 carbon steel will be soft during the adjustment but take special care to limit the bend to around 3°. As with the forged carbon steel adjusting the hosel further will introduce wrinkles into the chrome plating protecting the head.

Apply force using the gradual pressure method. The Thrust Rating is 3-5. The material provides the technician with plenty of feedback from a feel standpoint. More than 3° of adjustment can be made to an 8620 carbon steel iron if cosmetics are not a concern. As with the forged carbon steel the 8620 head will experience crinkles or wrinkling in the bend area where the chrome plating is stretched and compressed. If plating damage is not a concern you can bend the hosel up to 6°-8°.

Many of the 'rusty' type wedges of the past were produced from 8620 carbon steel. The chrome plating was never applied allowing the metal to either oxidize in dry conditions or rust in humid or dampness. There is no worry about chrome plating cracking on the hosel of these clubs. Adjustments can be made upwards of 8°.

Other Iron Materials

As previously stated many of the low cost irons are produced from die cast zinc or aluminum. Zinc is the most common of the two economical materials. Neither of these two materials have the ductility to accept a hosel bend. Trying to adjust these heads only 1° leads to catastrophic failure – broken hosels.

At the opposite end of the hardness spectrum are higher strength stainless steel irons. Unlike soft and brittle aluminum or zinc, high strength stainless steel has a small amount of ductility to it but can be extremely hard to adjust. 450 stainless steel has been used in irons by a few manufacturers in the late 1990's. Adjusting 450 stainless steel is a similar experience to adjusting non-heat treated 17-4 stainless steel, except you will be able to get a degree or two of adjustment without breaking the hosel. A Thrust Rating of 9-10 is necessary using a jerk execution. In addition to the 450 stainless, 15-5 stainless steel is rarely used for iron production. There have been 15-5 applications I have used for designs in the past. They bend similarly to 17-4 stainless steel.

On occasion you may run across irons cast out of beryllium copper. The most commonly produced model were the BeCu Ping Eye2 irons however many manufacturers rode on the success of Ping's coat tails with their own beryllium copper models. Beryllium copper is predominantly copper. Only 1%-3% of the alloy is actually beryllium. There is a slight amount of metal memory to the material. During my days working the PGA Tour the Ping Eye2 BeCu irons and wedges were in abundance. I was able to bend them in the same manner as 431 stainless steel. Due to the alloy properties 3° was pretty much the maximum bend. Thrust Rating is 5-7 and a gradual pressure method of bending is recommended.

Another material that has cropped up over the years are variations of bronze alloy. It hasn't been since the mid-1990's that a major manufacturer (Callaway) has introduced an aluminum bronze iron design. Shortly after Cleveland introduced their bronze wedges. The bronze alloy used in golf has similar bending characteristics to 304 stainless steel. Use a gradual pressure bending method where you'll experience a Thrust Rating of 4-6.

Both TaylorMade and Callaway introduced titanium/tungsten irons in the late 1990's. The main bodies of the irons were produced out of a 6-4 titanium alloy with a tungsten rear and sole weight used to stabilize the head on miss-hits. Most recently Callaway has manufactured their Fusion irons from a titanium body. If you have ever attempted to adjust the hosel of a 6-4 titanium driver you know the difficulties of working with the material. In the form of irons the 6-4 titanium is no different. Use the jerk method to orchestrate the bend. If successful you may be able to achieve 1°-2° of hosel adjustment. The Thrust Rating is 8-10 so a good deal of force is required to make an adjustment.

It is also possible to heat the hosel up red hot using a propane torch to execute a greater degree of adjustment. However a home heat treatment in the oven does not yield good enough results as the propane torch method for bending.

Material	Formed	Rockwell Hardness	Elongation	Maximum Safe Adjustment	Bending Method	Thrust Rating
6-4 Titanium	Cast	HRC35	10%	2°	Jerk	8 - 10
Non-Alloyed Titanium	Lathed	HRC23	15%	1°	Gradual	3 - 5
450 Stainless Steel	Cast	HRC28	13%	2°	Jerk	9 - 10
15-5 Stainless Steel	Cast	HRC40	14%	2°	Jerk	8 - 10
17-4 Stainless Steel	Cast	HRC35	15%	2°	Jerk	7 - 9
410 Stainless Steel	Forged	HRB95	20%	8°	Gradual	3 - 5
431 Stainless Steel	Cast	HRC22	20%	4°	Jerk-Grad	5 - 7
431-1/TTL Stainless Steel	Cast	HRC18	20%	10°	Jerk-Grad	5 - 7
304 Stainless Steel	Cast	HRB85	40%	10°	Gradual	3 - 6
1000 Series Carbon Steel	Foorged	HRB85	31%	4°	Gradual	3 - 5
8620 Carbon Steel (Plated)	Cast	HRB89	31%	4°	Gradual	3 - 5
8620 Carbon Steel (Non-Plated)	Cast	HRB89	31%	8°	Gradual	3 - 5
Beryllium Copper Alloy	Cast	HRB45	25%	3°	Jerk	6 - 8
Aluminum Bronze Alloy	Cast	HRB95	35%	8°	Gradual	4 - 6

There have been numerous clubs introduced that incorporate a stainless steel body with a titanium face insert. Many club technicians avoid bending these models in fear of warping the body to where the face insert will fall out. This is seldom a problem. Every titanium face iron I have designed is similar to what other manufacturers have done. The titanium face is swaged into the stainless steel body. I have been able to bend every hosel 2° and successfully pass air canon and robot durability testing following the adjustment of each new design.

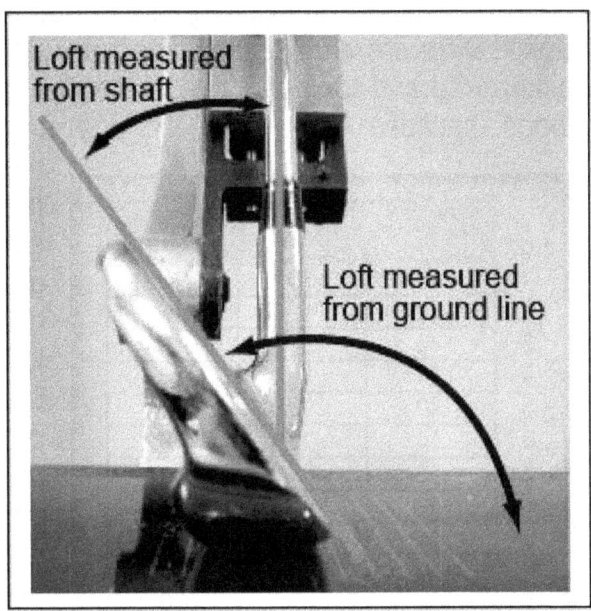

Limit hosel adjustments on titanium face irons to 2° and you will be safe. The next question is whether the body is 431 or 17-4 stainless steel. However it makes little difference since the recommended bend is limited to 2°.

In recent years new light density alloys have been introduced by some manufacturers, specifically for wedges. Cleveland introduced their CG10 material. This alloy cannot be bent as it is very brittle with little ductility to it. While offered as a premium product the hosels easily break when only 1° of adjustment is made to the club, much like the low cost zinc irons. Snake Eyes introduced a powdered metal light density alloy in their 650PM wedges that is capable of a 4° adjustment. Use the gradual pressure method to bend the hosel which will have a Thrust Rating of 4-6.

Cause and Effect Adjusting Irons

When adjusting irons there are typically two specifications you are looking to hit – the loft and the lie angles. With some adjustments you are only attempting to adjust one of these specifications. In others both the loft and lie angle require adjusting. I'll discuss both the individual approaches to each spec in addition to a single combination bend. Let us focus on the loft adjustment first.

The Objectives | Iron Loft Adjustments

Before adjusting an iron's loft it must first be measured. As with any specification adjustment you must know where you are at versus where you are taking the specs. Measuring loft is not as standardized as many golfers would think. Different club technicians take different approaches depending on their background and tools that are available. Irons tend to be easier to measure than woods because there isn't a face angle or roll factor to include in the measurement. Most clubmakers will measure iron loft in one of two ways; either off of the shaft or from the grounded sole plane. Measuring off of the shaft will provide the most accurate loft reading because it provides you with the golf club's truly effective loft. This procedure is the most relevant because the hands are controlling the clubhead through the shaft and it is that relationship which will dictate the ball flight. For instance, if the hands are pressed forward (which places the shaft angle forward too) the face-to-shaft angle relationship remain unchanged, however a face-to-ground relationship would now provide a stronger reading. Measuring from the ground is also viable however irons that incorporate an ample degree of positive or negative bounce can influence the reading. If a club as 2 degrees of bounce, the clubhead measurement will be 2 degrees less than in actuality. The opposite is true for negative bounce. In these instances it is very important that the loft measurement be taken with the clubface squared up perfectly and not in an open or closed face angle position that is influenced by the sole.

Iron	Average Lofts		
	Pre-1990	1990's	Current
1	17	16	15
2	20	18	17
3	23	21	20
4	26	24	23
5	30	28	26
6	34	32	30
7	38	36	34
8	42	40	38
9	46	44	42
P	50	48	46
S	56	56	56

For all of these reasons it is important to dynamically measure for loft. Loft is adjusted to help achieve a desired launch angle in addition to a specified yardage carry. But most importantly loft should be adjusted in order to keep a uniform yardage dispersion between each iron in the set. The typical golf club manufacturer incorporates 4° of loft between each of the mid and short irons. There is usually 1° less between the two longest irons. When evaluating the lofts within a set of irons the common approach is to space each iron's loft apart in the 3° or 4° standard increments so that the set mathematically looks correct on paper. Even the most experienced golf aficionado holds to these guidelines. However based on my years of custom fitting it is a proven fact that the 3°-4° loft incrimination does not lead to consistent yardages between each golfer's clubs. Most individuals expect to see a 10-12 yard increment between each of

Getting Bent

their irons. While this may be the case with some of their lofts it is seldom seen throughout the entire iron set. In fact based on the expertise of the golfer there tends to be a great disparity of distance between the mid and longer irons. With less skilled golfers there may be as few as 3-5 yards between the longer irons in the set while an expert ball striker may see over 15 yards disparity between the same clubs.

Iron	Loft	Degree Increments	Anticipated Yardage Dispersion	Average Dispersion 15 Handicap
3	20	3	10 - 12	3
4	23	3	10 - 12	4
5	26	3	10 - 12	8
6	30	4	10 - 12	9
7	34	4	10 - 12	10
8	38	4	10 - 12	10
9	42	4	10 - 12	10
P	46	4	10 - 12	

The primary objective in adjusting the lofts is to bring a distance consistency between each iron. This is accomplished best dynamically, either on the range or golf course, or in a hitting bay using a launch monitor. The important objective of this exercise is to be able to identify each of the yardages that the irons are being carried. Do not guess at the distances. Factual data is the objective.

Starting from the highest lofted wedge in the set the golfer should hit a few shots with every iron to determine the carry distance of each club. Three solid impacts will usually suffice per club. With the data recorded the necessary adjustments should be made to the lofts so that there is a consistent disparity in yardage between every iron. This is the ultimate objective when adjusting iron lofts.

Once a consistency in yardages between each club is achieved through loft adjustments it is interesting to note the final loft specifications. Quite often they will mathematically appear to be a bad set of specifications. However dynamically the results are exactly what the golfer is looking for – consistently predictable distances between every iron in the set.

The primary cause and effect of adjusting lofts is to achieve a consistency in yardage dispersion. However another effect from a loft adjustment is the bounce angle of the club's sole. There is a direct correlation between loft adjustments and the effect on the sole's bounce angle. For every degree that the loft specification is weakened the bounce angle of the sole is increased by the same number of degrees. For example if an iron had a loft of 43° and a bounce angle of 3°, increasing its loft 2° would result in a final loft of 45° with a 5° bounce angle.

Strengthening (or reducing) the loft results in the opposite effect. If that same iron had the loft strengthened 2° the new loft would be 41° with a bounce angle of 1°. It is important to understand the role of a club's sole bounce so you are aware of how the club's dynamics are changed when the bounce angle is altered. Bounce is further discussed in much further detail in the book *The Perfect Fit*.

The Execution — Iron Loft Adjustments

When adjusting only the loft specification of an iron it is important not to alter the lie angle if it is already set to the correct position. Special care should be taken in orienting the bending bar in the correct position to effectively change the loft without changing the lie.

When strengthening the loft (decreasing it) the hosel bend should be directed towards the rear of the head. This requires for the bending bar to be positioned in one of two orientations. The first option is to swing the bending bar into a position that is forward of the hosel. From this position an upwards force to the bar will bend the upper portion of the hosel more rearward. This reduces the angle between the face and the hosel thereby strengthening the club's loft.

The second option is to swing the bending bar into a position that is pointing rearward of the hosel. In this orientation a downward force is placed on the bending bar to strengthen the loft.

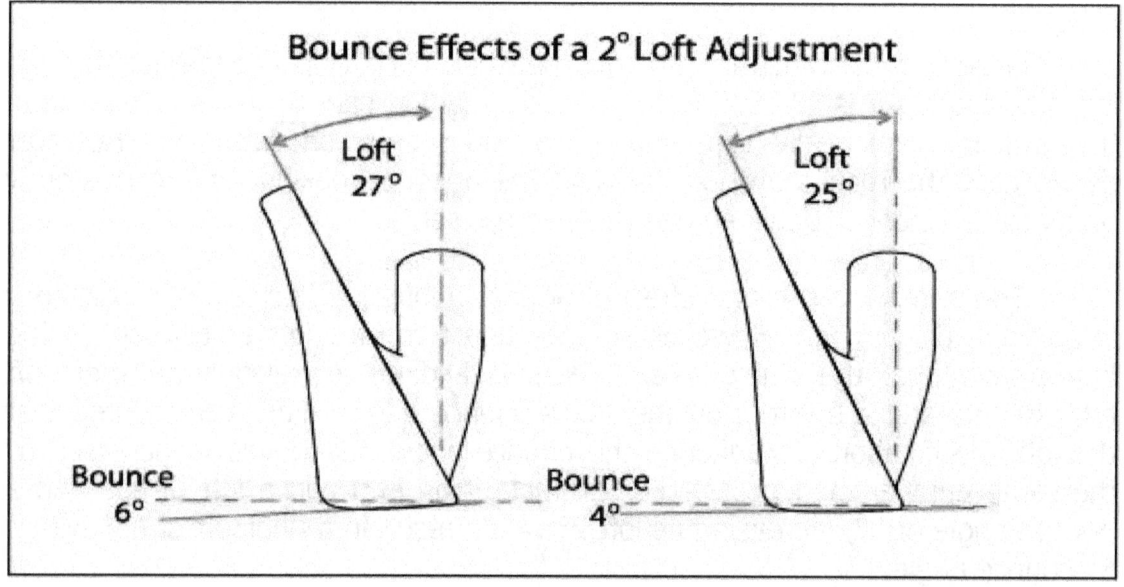

Only with experience you will be able to gauge the amount of force and movement required to make a specified adjustment. When making loft adjustments to a full set of irons you will find that not enough force is used on

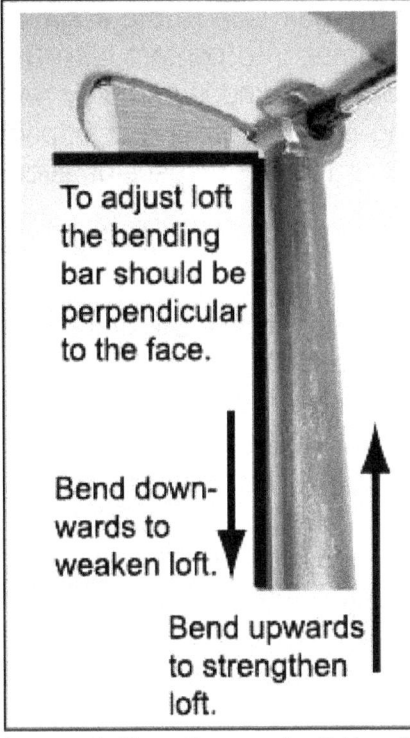

To adjust loft the bending bar should be perpendicular to the face.

Bend downwards to weaken loft.

Bend upwards to strengthen loft.

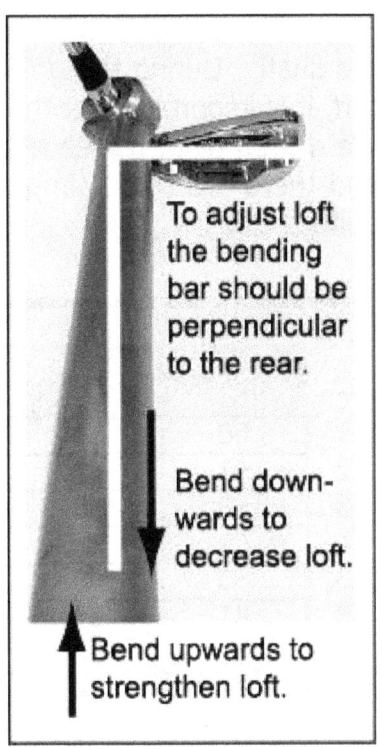

To adjust loft the bending bar should be perpendicular to the rear.

Bend downwards to decrease loft.

Bend upwards to strengthen loft.

some lofts to hit the target spec on the first try and too much force has been used on others. Adjusting hosels is all about feel the best way to hone your feel is through experience.

To weaken (increase) the loft of the iron an opposite force is applied. Again, with the first option having the bar pointing forward of the face, a downward force is used to weaken the loft. Remember, this is the opposite direction of force used to strengthen the loft.

The second option is to position the bending bar pointing rearward of the face. An upward force is then applied to weaken the loft.

Once an adjustment to the loft is made it is important to measure both the loft and the lie of the iron. You arbitrarily may have influenced the lie angle spec more upright or flatter while adjusting the loft. If this is the case then the lie angle must be adjusted back to its original specification.

The Objectives — Iron Lie Angle Adjustments

The golf club lie angle is the most important fitting specification that a golfer can be fit to. With so many individual specifications available for adjustment, there is always one spec that every custom fitting program incorporates into the process – fitting for the appropriate lie angle.

Lie Angle

The lie angle is the relationship of the sole of the golf club to the angle of the shaft. During the golf swing, as the club head comes into contact with the turf, it is important that the relationship of the sole to the ground is perfectly flat. We do not want to see either the toe or heel digging into the ground at impact and there are some simple approaches to take into fitting this aspect of every golfer's clubs.

Iron	Average Lie Angles		
	Pre-1990	1990's	Current
1	56	56	58
2	57	57	59
3	58	58	60
4	59	59	61
5	60	60	62
6	61	61	62.5
7	62	62	63
8	63	63	63.5
9	64	64	64
P	64	64	64
S	64	64	64

The relationship of the golf club's sole to the shaft is important because the lie angle influences the flight path of the golf ball. A lie angle that is too upright for one golfer may be too flat for another. Therefore adjusting the golf club's lie angle is an important element to obtaining the correct fit for a consistency in ball flight and determining predictable ball flight direction.

As a golfer swings a golf club and the head makes contact with the ball, the lie angle relationship will determine if the ball will be projected in a direction that will be straight, right or left. For a perfectly struck shot, a golf club with the correct lie angle will send the ball on a straight trajectory. However if the lie angle were to be too flat, a perfectly struck golf shot will have a tendency to fade or slice the ball, depending on the golf club's loft. The greater the loft (i.e., shorter irons and wedges) the greater the influence of sidespin to the ball for an ill fit lie angle. The opposite is true if the lie angle is too upright. A perfectly struck shot will either draw, or if the loft is high enough, hook. The importance of identifying and setting the correct lie angle to a golfer's clubs is the first step on the path towards a properly fit set of clubs.

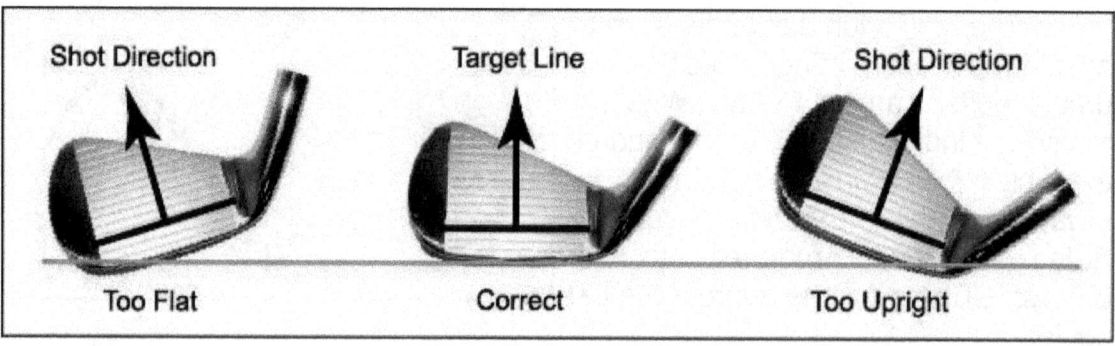

Another issue with an incorrect lie angle pertains to the heel or toe digging into the turf and interrupts what may otherwise be a clean shot. In some instances as the heel digs into the turf first it can abruptly shut the face of the club causing the ball to pull or pull/hook. When the toe digs into the ground it can leave the clubface open thereby creating a push or push/fade. These are extreme circumstances, usually in side hill or deep rough situations.

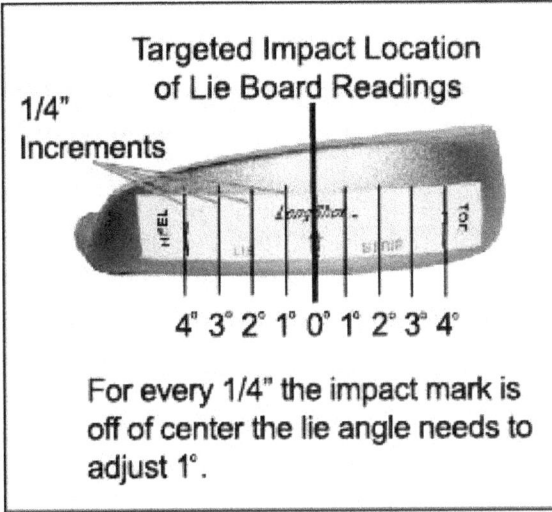

For every 1/4" the impact mark is off of center the lie angle needs to adjust 1°.

The lie angle specification for a golfer can easily be identified using a lie angle impact board. Using either the golfer's own clubs or a fitting club the golfer will hit balls from the impact board's surface. Tape on the sole of the club identifies the impact location between the iron's sole and board. If the impact location is in the center of the sole the club's lie angle is good for that golfer. However if the impact is located off-center, either towards the heel or the toe, the tape will identify that off-center impact point. Regular masking tape can be used or specialized impact tape is also available for this exercise. The lie angle of the club will need to be adjusted in order for the center of the sole to become the impact location with the board.

For every 1/4" that the impact point is located off-center a 1° lie angle adjustment must be made for that iron to properly fit the golfer's swing. For example, let's say the golfer hits some shots off the impact board and the contact location on the sole is 1/2" towards the heel from the sole's center. The heel-ward impact point indicates that the lie angle is too upright for the golfer. Therefore the lie angle needs to be bent flatter. With the impact location 1/2" from the center the lie angle would need to be adjusted 2° flatter on the current iron. The opposite would be true if the impact location was toe-ward instead.

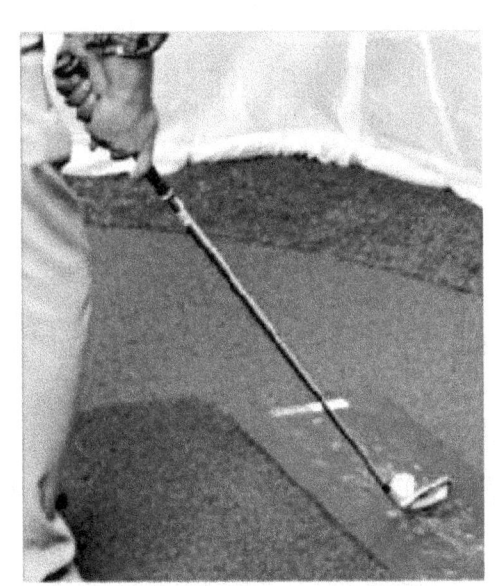

Using a lie angle impact board.

When running through an iron fitting many clubfitters alter their protocol on what they see as the perfect fit for the golfer. However there is one element that is universal from the most skilled to the least experienced fitter – the dynamic fitting of the lie angle is one of the most important fitting elements.

The Execution — Adjusting Iron Lofts & Lies

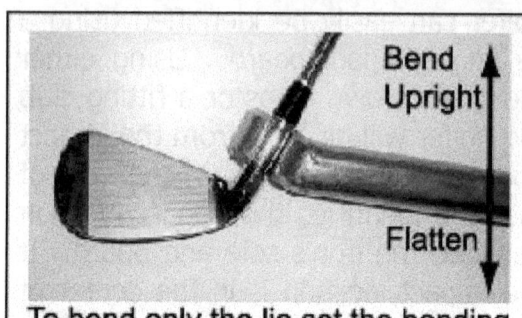

To bend only the lie set the bending bar on a parallel plane to the face of the iron.

Adjusting the hosel to the correct lie angle is slightly less complicated than adjusting for loft. There is only one position that the bending bar should be in to adjust the lie angle. Orientate the bending bar so it is pointing away from the heel side of the club. Visualize the bar on a parallel plane to the scorelines on the iron's face. With the bar in this position you can make a lie angle adjustment without affecting the iron's loft specification.

A downward force on the bending bar will flatten the lie angle. An upward force changes the iron's lie angle to a more upright position. As long as the bending bar is kept on a parallel path to the scorelines during the bend only the lie spec will be affected.

As with loft, sometimes the lie angle adjustment either under or overshoots its target. It is important to measure the angle during the adjustment to ensure it is achieved. At the same time verify that you have not accidently altered the loft. If it was changed then adjust it back to its proper specification.

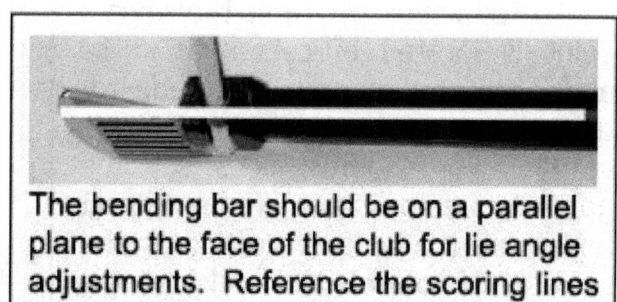

The bending bar should be on a parallel plane to the face of the club for lie angle adjustments. Reference the scoring lines for alignment.

The Execution — Compound Bends of Iron Lofts & Lies

If both the loft and lie angles require adjustment to hit the appropriate target specs it is possible to execute the adjustment using a single bend. You will find that it takes some experience getting used to the feel of different types of metal and head designs to bend to your target spec on the first try. Quite often you will have not bent the hosel enough or find yourself adjusting past the target spec. Only time and experience will turn you into a fine tuned club technician capable of hitting all specs on the first attempt. The fact is even the most experienced technicians will miss hitting some of the target specs on the first try.

It is possible to execute a 2-for-1 adjustment to the hosel where both the loft and lie require changes. This is achieved through the proper orientation of the hosel. Where experience is necessary to learn the appropriate feel for the proper amount of bending force, a greater amount of experience will help guide the technician to the correct bending bar position and force for a combination adjustment.

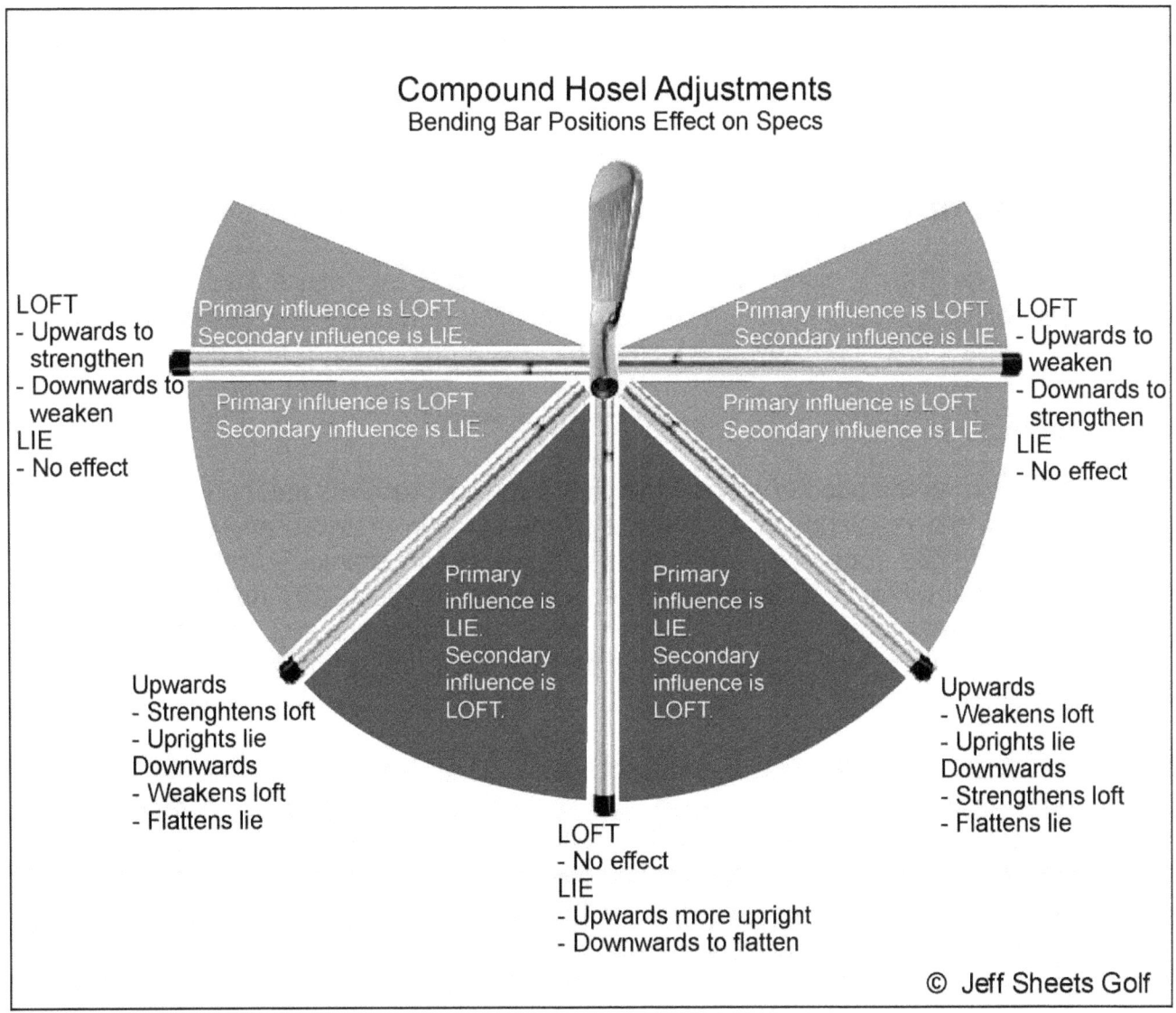

So far we have focused on three primary bar positions to bend loft and lie. With the bar extended either forward or rearward of the face the loft can be adjusted. As the bar is extended outward from the heel the lie angle can be adjusted. These are the three primary bar positions. Compound adjustments can be made to the hosel by orientating the bar to the non-primary positions. The term compound refers to a bend that adjusts both the loft and lie angle in the same motion.

As the bending bar is swung between the primary positions varying degrees of influence can be applied to the adjustment of the loft and lie. Take a look at the Compound Hosel Adjustments chart. With the toe of the iron pointing towards 12 o'clock the three primary bending bar positions are at 3:00, 6:00 and 9 o'clock. With the bending bar slightly off-plane of the 3:00 or 9:00 position a compound adjustment is made with greater influence to the loft and less with the lie. However both specifications will be altered with the bar in this position. For example, if the bending bar is positioned at 8 o'clock, an upwards thrust would strengthen the loft. At the same time the lie angle would flatten very slightly. As the bar is swung closer to 6 o'clock there is a greater influence on the lie angle and less on the loft.

Summarizing Iron Adjustments

Just like the game of golf itself, practice and experience lead to better hosel bending results. While it can be challenging to teach a new golfer the feel and sensations of perfectly struck shots there is a quick way to help develop the proper feel for bending different types of steel and titanium hosels. Some sacrificial club heads will be required for this exercise.

During the bend of a hosel the club technician receives feedback from the metal by the resistance or acceptance to the bending pressure applied. When bending forged irons, soft carbon steel castings or soft stainless steel heads the feedback is rather fluid feeling and easy to sense. The higher ductility of the softer metals makes bending the hosel a quick learning process. It is with the harder metals where sensory on the part of the club technician needs to be developed.

How does one sense if a stubborn hosel bend is going to accept the force you're applying to it or will resist and snap in two? I have found that the quickest way towards developing this feel it by over-shooting your adjustment goal. Developing this feel happens immediately when you purposely snap off the hosel to a stubborn material. Pursue this exercise by purchasing inexpensive cast irons from garage sales, swap meets and other such venues. Collecting an assortment of different iron models will provide a variety of different feels and feedback as you attempt to bend each hosel to its breaking point. A couple of things happen during this hosel breaking exercise. The first, a sense of the amount of force required to bring the club to its breaking point for each different type of metal. You will find that you will eventually care less what type of steel you are trying to adjust. Its feel is all you'll need to initially guide you on the amount of force to use.

The second factor to note in breaking the hosel from the head is the sensation of the snap. Many golf club technicians are startled when they accidently bend a hosel to its breaking point. In some cases it is like unexpectedly popping a balloon. There's no danger or pain involved but it can be a shocking if you're not expecting it. Once you have purposefully broken enough hosels you will have developed a good feel for the appropriate amount of force you can apply to a stubborn bend. I have found this approach to be the quickest way to developing your sensory skills and confidence in adjusting iron hosels.

Loft & Lie Adjustments for Woods

Most golf club technicians do not get involved with adjusting the loft and lie angles on woods. Namely because there have not been a lot of wood bending machines with much versatility to them. For starters, bending titanium drivers is a difficult challenge. Trying to keep up with the quickly evolving growth of the driver head volume is discouragement enough. Metalwood bending machines have needed to grow at the same rate as driver heads over the past few years. There haven't been many club technicians wanting to purchase new bending units to keep up with the growing driver pace.

This metalwood bending unit handles oversize drivers in addition to fairway and hybrid woods.

Another reason for fewer loft and lie adjustments to woods are due to their lower lofts. The need for lie angles to be perfectly fit to a golfer is minimized when the golf club's loft is less than 25°. If you recall, the higher the loft, the greater the impact of the lie angle dynamics. The majority of woods have lofts stronger than 25°.

Many club technicians are not familiar with the procedure to change loft on a metalwood. It is quite simple however there is the basic need of having a metalwood bending machine. There are few commercially available metalwood bending units for sale. When researching the purchase of one determine the flexibility of the tool. Can it only bend fairway and hybrid woods or can the unit also accommodate drivers? What is the maximum size of driver it will hold? Is the unit only capable of securing the head in place or can you also take measurements of the head once it is locked into place? Companies like Mitchell Golf and Golfsmith have sold metalwood benders off and on over the years. However with the constantly changing geometry of drivers these days it has been a challenge for these specialty companies to keep up with the changing needs.

In recent years Golfsmith upgraded their iron loft & lie bending machines to accommodate hybrids woods. If there are any woods worth adjusting, hybrids are definitely good candidates. Because so many models have lofts reaching upwards of 30° and higher the need to adjust lie angles can be satisfied.

Our first focus on metalwood hosel adjustments will be towards materials. Some metalwoods are conducive to adjusting while others are just plain stubborn.

Titanium

Investment cast 6-4 titanium has always been a challenge to adjust. The only way to successfully cold bend a 6-4 hosel is in a fixture that has been customized for the specific head being bent. Many of the OEMs have created clamshell casings in which the titanium driver head is sandwiched into a 2-piece holder that engulfs the driver's body while allowing the hosel to protrude out of its casing. The casing is then placed into a fixture that holds it securely. The club technician can then use a jerk method to force the hosel into its desired position. All stresses on the ultra-thin shell of the driver are equally dispersed throughout the body so that the crown, skirt or sole do not collapse from the force. Such a fixture is not available to most club technicians who see a wide variety of different club head models for adjustment.

If you have a way of securing the driver for bending there is only one method available to non-OEM technicians – heat. As discussed with 17-4 stainless steel irons you can heat the hosel red hot and execute the bend on an investment cast 6-4 titanium driver hosel. Unlike a stainless steel iron which requires a polishing job after the adjustment, the titanium driver will require both a polish and a paint job to bring it back to its unblemished state. Most club technicians will not want to go through the effort of repainting a head for the sake of adjusting the hosel. I have done it many times in the past for PGA touring professionals but we're talking about a completely different clientele in this case. (Not to mention I had a separate painting department handle the refinishing after the heads were heated up.)

Aside from the investment cast 6-4 titanium drivers there are also many stamped titanium heads on the market. Unlike the 6-4 heads where both the entire body and hosel are made of the same material the stamped heads may be comprised of multiple types of titanium blends. This fact can lead to questionable material composition. With a stamped titanium driver the face is typically constructed from either 6-4 titanium or a beta titanium alloy. These are the strongest materials used in the stamped head construction. It is also common to produce the hosel out of 6-4 titanium. The most common crown material for stamped titanium drivers is 3-2 titanium. Quite often if the hosel is not manufactured out of 6-4 titanium then 3-2 titanium is used. Both of these materials can be a challenge to adjust.

Many of the driver designs I have developed the past few years use commercially pure titanium (grade 4) for the hosel instead of a titanium alloy. The pure titanium is much easier to adjust. Hosels constructed from pure titanium will easily accept a 1° adjustment without any problem. The Thrust Factor is 3-5 so there is minimal resistance to the bend. Use a gradual pressure to adjust the hosel because going up to 2° or beyond will likely result in its breaking.

So what are the indicators of the titanium driver's construction? Resistance to the bend is the sign. Drivers constructed from 6-4 titanium or similarly strong alloys will be a challenge to get any type of hosel adjustment without using intense heat. Very few models incorporate the softer pure titanium hosels I like to use in my designs. Place a bending bar on the hosel and use gradual pressure to see if it moves. If this does not happen immediately then you are likely dealing with a titanium alloy. The alloys will require heat, which you should only pursue if you are willing to refinish a charred paint job on the head.

Some fairway woods are also manufactured out of titanium. The same principals apply to the titanium fairway woods as the titanium drivers. Some are cast in 6-4 titanium alloy while others are constructed from 4-piece stampings. Take the same approach with a titanium fairway wood as you would a titanium driver. There is not likely a need to deal with titanium-based hybrid woods.

However if any were to come onto the market the same considerations should be applied based on the hybrid's manufacturing method.

Do not be fooled by the marketing used by some golf manufacturers when it comes to materials. Some companies may state that their drivers are constructed from beta titanium however beta titanium is never used anywhere in the body except for the face, and in some rare instances, the crown. Take the same approach to adjusting the hosel as you would an investment cast or 4-piece stamping.

Stainless Steel

Metalwoods constructed from stainless steel will usually be cast in the 17-4 variety. The 431 and 304 stainless steel used in irons is not durable enough for the thin walled hollow construction of metalwoods. This is particularly true of fairway woods however I have developed a few models of 431 stainless steel hybrid woods with success from the durability end.

Since all drivers have exploded to the 460cc size it is difficult to find one manufactured out of stainless steel anymore. The largest steel driver head I ever developed was 385cc. It raised eyebrows at the USGA because no one had ever submitted a steel driver of that size to them. However designers have pushed the design envelope with 460cc titanium drivers and have abandoned the much smaller stainless steel models which literally stopped selling. With this said, stainless steel metalwoods today are limited to fairway and hybrid woods.

17-4 stainless steel is the perfect alloy for fairway and hybrid woods. Since the head volumes are significantly smaller than drivers there is much that can be done from the design aspect in stainless steel. As for adjust ability a heat treated 17-4 stainless steel wood is capable of being bent 2°. As with irons a 17-4 wood that has not been heat treated will not want to bend at all. The hosel will break off before it will accept an adjustment.

Even if the hosel is heated up with a propane torch a maximum bend of 2° should be the limit. As the metalwood's hosel is being bent there is a great deal of stress surrounding the base of the hosel. The hosel is much thicker than the walls of the club at its base. Even if heat is used to make the material more pliable the thinner walls surrounding the hosel will not be able to handle the stretching and compression of a hosel being bent beyond 2°.

Another material that is less common in stainless wood construction is 15-5 stainless steel. The material properties of 15-5 are slightly stronger than 17-4, however most manufacturers prefer to work with the latter. Its ease of manufacturing and finishing make it the preference to most investment casting foundries. Another cast able higher strength steel is 450 stainless. It is stronger than both the 17-4 and 15-5 alloys.

A jerk method is recommended for adjusting 17-4, 15-5 and 450 stainless steel hosel. The Thrust Rating for these materials is 7-9. Restrict the adjustment to 2°. Anything beyond can break the hosel from the wood's body.

Some metalwoods are advertised as being produced from maraging steel, high strength steel such as Carpenter 455 or Tour Alloy 275 or 17-7 stainless. In each of these cases the material mentioned is only used in the wood's face. The bodies continue to be 17-4 stainless steel so the bending protocols for 17-4 are used.

The Objectives — Adjusting Wood Lie Angles

During the years I worked on the PGA Tour, fewer than 10% of the professionals I built clubs for had a lie angle requirements for their fairway woods, and about 25% had specific lie angle needs for their drivers (this was back in the pre-titanium driver days). However 100% had lie angle specifications established for their irons. As drivers evolved from stainless steel to titanium fewer drivers have been designed to be adjusted leaving most of today's touring professionals using "standard" lie angle specs. Basically meaning when it comes to a wood's lie angle - it is what it is. Many cannot be adjusted without special equipment and follow up services (namely, refinishing).

Adjusting lie angles for stainless steel woods is still possible when using the right equipment. As with the irons, the appropriate bending equipment is necessary to bend the hosel successfully. Namely, a bending unit that can hold the head firmly so that the hosel can be adjusted accordingly. Heat treatment plays an important role in the adjustment of stainless steel woods. Without proper heat treatment, many stainless woods experience stress risers at the base of the hosel, more commonly towards the crown than the heel. It is in this area where the metal will fracture if adjusted beyond the point that the metal's ductility will allow. Experience pays off as the biggest factor in bending metal woods just like it is with many cast irons. The club technician has a feel for the metal and knows when it is resisting the adjustment more stubbornly than other heads. Breaking a few hosels always leads to a better feel for adjusting lie angles.

When adjusting the hosels on woods there are three specifications that are typically considered – loft, lie and face angle. What most club technicians do not realize is that loft and face angle of the wood go hand-in-hand. As the face angle is adjusted so is the loft specification. The lie angle is independent on its own.

Let's discuss the lie angle first. Because a driver, fairway or hybrid wood has so little loft on it the lie angle is almost an inconsequential specification that needs to be dealt with. Starting with the driver, this is a club where the golf ball is teed up. The sole of the club should theoretically not come in contact with the ground. Because of these factors there really is not a need to adjust the driver's lie angle. Even with the droop factor coming into play most driver lie angle specs have taken the shaft bend into account. Measuring for a lie angle spec with a teed up shot isn't feasible so rarely will you see the lie angle specs of a driver addressed.

When it comes to fairway woods and hybrids you can execute a dynamic lie angle fitting by hitting golf balls off of an impact board. After working through numerous fittings you will realize that the lie angle of these clubs only becomes important when the loft of the head exceeds 25°. This is a fact realized more by watching ball flight as opposed to viewing only the impact tape on the wood's sole. Few fairway woods have lofts higher than 25° however it is becoming more common to find hybrid clubs with the higher lofts.

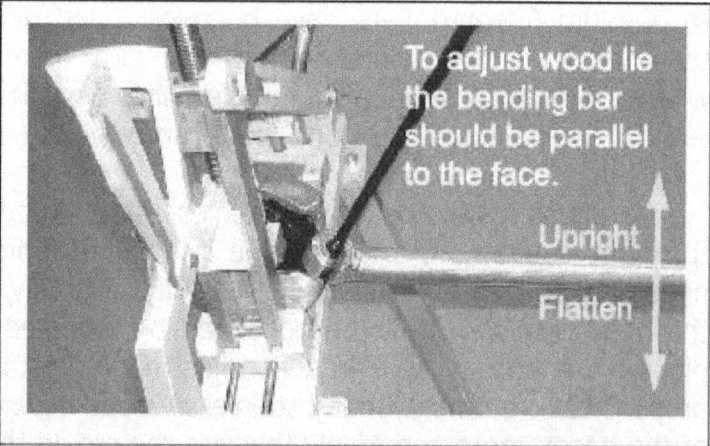

The lie angle adjustment should be executed by aligning the bending bar parallel to the face of the wood. This is the same approach taken with bending an iron's lie angle. Make the adjustment by moving the bending bar directly upward or downward depending on the desired specification. Adjusting a wood's lie angle will also provide a minor effect on the ball's trajectory. More upright lie angles will generally launch the ball slightly higher whereas flatter lie angles will provide a slightly lower trajectory. These trajectory changes are slight nuances and can sometimes only be identifiable using a launch monitor to capture the launch conditions data.

Cause and Effect — Adjusting Wood Loft & Face Angles

Opening or closing the face angle to a particular spec is the most common request club technicians receive concerning metalwood hosel adjustments. What most golfers and many technicians do not realize is that there is a 1:1 effect on loft when the face angle is moved. For every degree that the face angle is opened the loft of the driver strengthens a degree. The opposite is true for closing the face angle. Every degree it is close increases the wood's dynamic loft. It is through the face angle adjustment that the dynamic loft of the driver is altered.

Many golfers do not understand the dynamics of face angle adjustment affecting loft. In fact, many believe the opposite is true. For these dynamics to play out correctly we must make one primary assumption – that when the golfer goes to hit the ball with the wood the intent is to have the face squared up to the target line at impact. To understand the face angle/loft dynamics we'll take a look at a driver adjustment.

Scenario 1: Loft – 12°   Face Angle – Square

We'll begin with a 12° lofted driver that has a square face angle. If the request is to bend its face angle 2° closed the hosel will be shifted into a more forward position to accomplish this. Placing the newly adjusted driver onto a loft/lie measurement unit there are two different approaches that can be taken to measure its loft. The first is to square up the club face in the gauge and measure the face's loft angle from the ground line. With the face in the square position a 14° reading is made. This is the face angle most golfers will attempt to have the head oriented during impact.

A second reading for the loft can be pursued by allowing the face to sit 2° closed in the loft/lie measurement gauge. With the face 2° closed a protractor reading between the face and the ground line will read the original 12° loft spec. For the golfer to achieve a higher trajectory from the newly adjusted driver the face must be squared up at impact. If the golfer impacts the ball with the face 2° closed it will come off the clubface with its original trajectory, but on a path left of the target line (for a right handed golfer).

Scenario 2: Loft – 10° Face Angle – Square

The opposite scenario works when opening up the face angle. Let's begin with a 10° driver. For simplicity sake it too starts out with a square face angle. The golfer has asked for it to be opened 2°. In order to make the adjustment it is best to orientate the bending bar in a forward position of the face. The bar is forced in the direction towards the driver's golf shaft thereby bending the hosel back and opening the face angle.

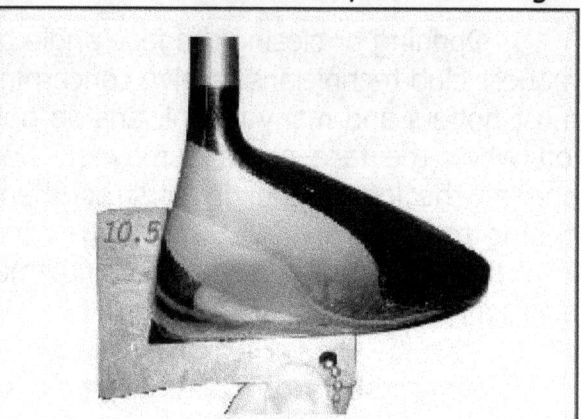

Face-to-sole gages are inaccurate. They only identify the face-to-sole angle - not the dynamic loft angle. As the hosel angle is bent the face-to-sole angle never changes, but the loft dynamics do change.

As the driver is placed into the measurement gauge with its new face angle laying open at 2° the loft measurement is still 10°. As the face is rotated back to a square position the face's loft angle decreases. As it is measured in the square position the driver's new loft reads 8°. Intended use of the driver is to impact the ball with the face square where its dynamic loft is now 8°. However if you were to measure the loft using a sole-to-face gauge you will note that the loft angle never changed using this antiquated tool. The proper way to measure a wood's loft is the ground line-to-face relationship since this represents the interaction that will be experienced between the club and the ball.

These scenarios which begin with square face angles are easy to understand. Let's study on additional scenario where we begin with a closed face angle on the driver.

Scenario 3: Loft – 9° Face Angle – 2° Open

The driver to be adjusted has 9° of loft with a 2° open face angle. Before proceeding any further the loft and face angle relationship need to be clarified. There are two different ways to interpret 9° of loft and a 2° open face angle. The two previous scenarios the face angle specs started out square. When beginning with an open or closed face angle a determination needs to be made on how the manufacturer based the loft.

It must be determined if the 9° of loft is measured with the face in a squared position or measured with it sitting in its 2° open position. Based on the measurement method the driver will have on of two completely different dynamic lofts.

If the 9° of loft was specified by the manufacture based on a square measurement position then the loft will read 11° as it is rotated to its 2° open position.

However if the manufacturer's loft specification was based on an 9° measurement with the face open 2° it will measure 7° in a square position.

In either case the two different loft reference methods result in completely different dynamic lofts when compared to one another in a square face angle position. Most golfers will easily notice a difference in the launch angle between drivers with a 7° and 11° dynamic lofts.

Scenario 4: Making the driver look square!

When it comes to adjusting the hosel on a driver (or any fairway wood) it must be determined what the golfer's desire really is when requesting the club to be bent. Is it a desire for a different face angle or an alteration to the loft? My experience is that the face angle can be equally as important as the amount of loft on a driver to many golfers.

Here we have a scenario where the golfer has requested that the face angle be opened so that the face appears to be square at setup. Here's a little known fact: For a wood to *look* square at setup its face angle needs to be approximately ½° open. Allow .5° addition opening of the face angle spec for any golfer seeking a square face. I've bent the face angles of woods for many touring professionals who requested a square face angle. In each event I had to verify if they were seeking a zero degree face angle measurement or a "square look." The objective usually was the square look which meant opening the face as oppose to squaring it up.

Measuring wood lofts and face angles can be confusing for many technicians, based on the different measurement methods available. However the technician must completely understand them in order to hit target specifications properly. I personally recommend referencing all lofts from the square face angel position. Unfortunately this is not an industry standard practice primarily for marketing purposes.

A good example of this is the need for more loft for the average golfer. Today's large high tech driver heads perform better in higher lofts than the smaller metalwoods of the past. Yet most equipment manufacturers find it easiest to sell drivers with lofts ranging from 9° - 10.5° on their soleplates. The manufacturers know that the majority of recreational golfers should be playing with at least 11.5° - 13.5° of loft in their drivers. To help get the proper loft into a golfer's hands some manufacturers' loft specifications are based on the face angle spec. You have learned here the relationships of loft and face angle. A driver can have a 10.5° loft based on either a square face measurement or a face angle measurement. If the 10.5° is the result of a measurement with the face angle 2.5° closed we know that a dynamic loft measurement of 13° will result once the face is measured at a square position. What is being sold to the consumer is a driver with 13° of loft but marketed as a 10.5° driver. There is truth in the loft marking of the sole but it is nevertheless a somewhat deceptive practice.

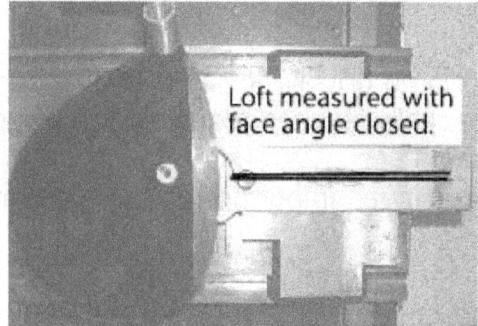

Loft Measured on Face Angle Spec

Loft measured with face angle closed.

Face Angle @ 1.25 closed = 11 loft

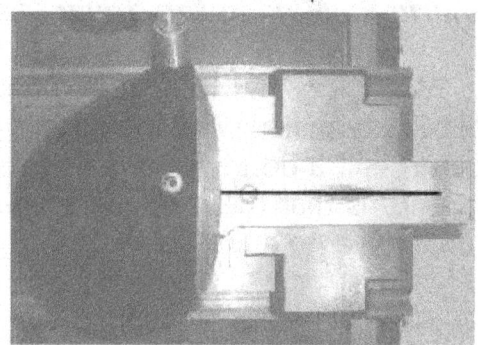

Loft Measured with Square Face

Face Angle @ 0 = 11 loft

A driver's measured loft can lead to confusion based on how it has been measured. It is easier to compare wood specifications by referencing all loft measurements based on a square face angle.

By measuring all woods with the face angle in the square position you will be able to identify the correct dynamic loft of the clubhead. Face angle is very important and in many cases will be the driving force of a hosel bend request. Yet the golf club is intended to be used with the face in a square position at impact for most shots so all loft measurements should be made with a zero degree face angle.

A great amount of focus has been on the driver, yet every variable spoken about here is also applicable to the fairway and hybrid woods. There is a greater variation on driver face angles than there are on fairway and hybrid woods. As the loft increases in fairway and hybrids woods the face angle specification tends to be square. Due to the difficulty that many golfers have with drivers has led to their varied face angle specifications.

The Execution — Adjusting Wood Lie Angles

As with iron lie angle adjustments the bending bar should be positioned outward from the hosel. It should be on the same plane as the scorelines on the wood's face. To flatten the lie angle a downward force is placed on the bending bar. Upward force is used on the bar for a more upright adjustment. There will be a much greater resistance to bending if the head is cast from 6-4 titanium. There is very much likelihood that heat from a propane torch is necessary to execute the bend. Just keep in mind that the club will likely need to be repainted if the body is scorched by the heat.

There will be very little resistance to bending if the hosel is constructed of commercially pure titanium. Very little force is necessary, so it is recommended to begin with gradual pressure instead of a jerk force for all titanium woods in determining the hosel material.

You will likely know that you are adjusting a stainless steel hosel based on the type of head being bent. All oversized drivers are manufactured from titanium however the vast majority of fairway and hybrid woods are cast from 17-4 stainless steel. If you are adjusting a fairway wood and it is titanium then take the same precautions you would use with a titanium driver. First gradual pressure followed by a jerk force if the hosel doesn't immediately bend.

Stainless steel is going to provide resistance to the pressure placed on the hosel bend. For a stronger individual a gradual pressure can be applied however a jerk force works well for most technicians.

Limit the bend to 2° with stainless steel woods. Even though the head has been heat treated and you can feel the metal accepting the bend there is a good likelihood of cracking through the thin crown area surrounding the base of the hosel by going beyond the 2° adjustment. Over my career I have broken more wood hosels than iron hosels yet the number of irons I have adjusted greatly outnumber the woods. In almost every case the wood hosel cracked on its crown side where the metal is very thin.

The Execution — Adjusting Wood Loft & Face Angles

The same principals guiding iron loft bending applies to woods also. The position of the bending bar is going to be oriented either forward towards the target line or rearward facing away from it. Executing the hosel bend is going to be similar to the loft adjustment bends for an iron. For example, with the bending bar facing forward, parallel to the target line, an upwards force to the bending bar is going to shove the hosel into a rearward slant. This opens the club face. On an iron it has an immediate impact on the hosel-to-face relationship by decreasing the iron's loft. On a wood however it opens the face angle which is a direct correlation to the loft angle. Depending on the bending bar design a downward force may be possible to close the face angle. However this is dependent on the type of bending bar-to-knuckle design. Some bending bars protrude directly off the equator of the knuckle other bar designs can be angled. To close the face angle it may be necessary to rotate the bending bar 180° towards the rear of the club and then an upward angle can more easily be applied to it to shut the face closed.

As with bending lie angles on woods it is not recommended to go beyond a 2° face angle adjustment. The same strains to the thin walled crown at the base of the hosel occur and snapping of the hosel can take place even when you can feel the metal accepting the bend.

One little trick to keeping ensuring you adjust only the face angle and not the lie at the same time is to keep the bending bar on a parallel plane to the target line (based on the wood's face angle). This is most easily accomplished

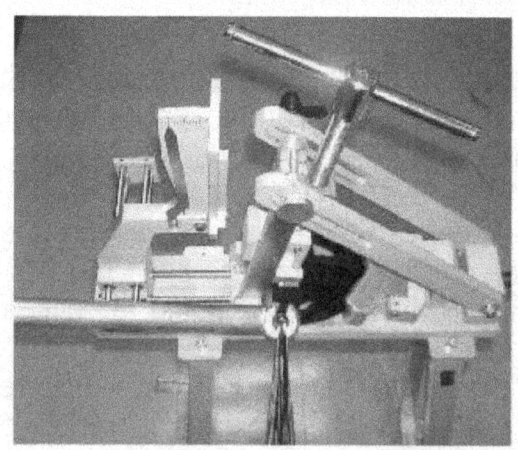 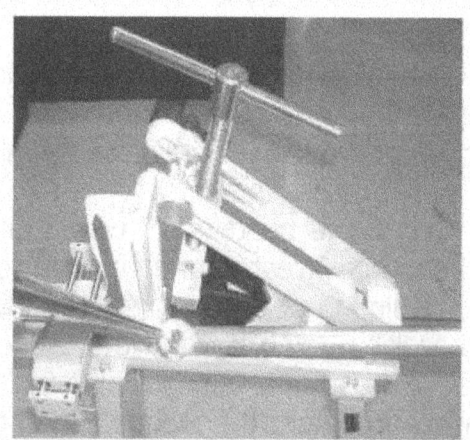

The face angle (and loft) are altered with the bending bar in a forward or rearward orientation to the face. Force the bar in the direction of the shaft to open the face angle (left photo). Likewise, force the bar in the direction of the shaft to close the face angle (right photo).

Effects of Face Angle Adjustments on Loft

The driver we begin with has a square face angle that registers "0" on the face angle gage.

The driver measures 10 degrees loft set in a square position.

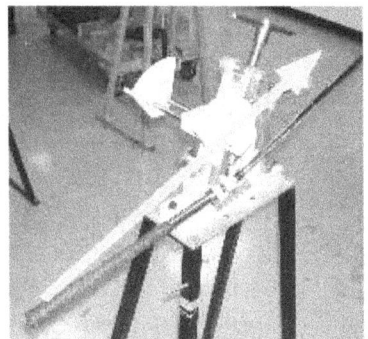

As the head is placed in a metalwood bender the hosel is bent rearward to open the face angle. It is moved 2° in the direction towards the shaft.

When the driver is placed back in the gage it sits 2° open instead of square.

The driver still measures 10° in the 2° open position.

At this point the driver is rolled closed back to a square reading of 0°. As the face is rolled closed the face angle is de-lofted. Upon measuring the squared face the lower loft reading of 8° is observed.

by placing force on the bending bar a plane with the shaft. Rotating the bar pointing more upward or downward affects both the face angle and lie. Visualize the bending bar and shaft on the same plane and force the bending bar in the direction of the shaft on that plane to ensure only the face angle is affected.

Compound Bends for Wood Loft/Face Angle/Lie Adjustments

If you recall the Compound Hosel Adjustment chart on page 23 there are three primary planes on which either loft/face angle or lie are adjusted. Drivers, fairway woods and hybrids utilize these same three planes for hosel adjustments to them. With the bending bar in a forward or rearward position only the face angle/loft of the wood is affected. By swinging the bending bar away from the head pointing away from the heel the lie angle can be adjusted. Using the space in between these three positions provides a compound bend to the hosel affecting both face angle (loft) and lie.

Most irons have a little bit better resiliency towards hosel adjustments. The wall thicknesses of the hosels are ample and most irons can have their hosels adjusted repeatedly without harming the club's durability. Woods are not so forgiving. This is why it is important to try minimizing the number of bends to a metalwood. As with the iron the hosel is plenty thick. However, as previously mentioned, the wall thickness surrounding the base of the hosel is extremely thin. Increasing the number of hosel adjustments weakens these thin walls so executing a compound bend is recommended if both face angle and lie need to be adjusted.

Refer to the Compound Hosel Adjustment chart for anticipating the most efficient hosel bend to affect both specifications.

Summarizing Wood Adjustments

Working towards the right feel of the bend for woods can be accomplished in a similar manner to irons. By adjusting numerous hosels to their maximum bend point a club technician can begin to get a good feel for the material. However I have found that there is a great variety of feel differences in the bending of metalwood hosels. First of all there is a vast different just between cast 6-4 titanium versus commercial grade titanium. Steel adds another layer of feel difference and then finally there are the head designs themselves.

Between the late 1990's and early 2000's many wood designs, drivers especially, utilized much shorter hosel lengths. This was done to redistribute as much weight as possible down into the head. Hosel lengths have crept back up to longer lengths permitting bending bar knuckles to grasp them much more easily. The longer the hosel the more real estate the club technician has to manipulate a hosel bend.

You may want to attempt the exercise of breaking hosels as I recommended for irons. Obtaining inexpensive metalwoods is a more challenging task than purchasing old irons for this cause. Where most irons are purchased in complete sets you will find yourself acquiring metalwoods a club at a time. This is more costly especially if purchasing titanium woods. Nevertheless it is a good practice to clue you into the necessary feel and bending force quickly. Besides, you can recycle all of the broken metalwoods as doorstops or paperweights.

Remember to protect the hosel from marring or scratching if necessary. Many wood hosels have been masked near the hosel opening so there is unpainted metal in its upper portion. If this is where the bending bar knuckle will rest there isn't much damage the bar can do during the adjustment. In many cases either the entire hosel is painted or the paint protrudes from the body and partially up the hosel. Note on whether or not the bending bar infringes into the painted area. If so a thin piece of leather or lead tape can be wrapped around the painted area so that the bending bar's knuckle will not scratch up the paint. Adjusting a wood hosel does not take much time at all, but if you have to refinish the wood with a new paint job because the paint was damaged during the bend you have just prolonged a relatively simple task.

Loft & Lie Adjustments for Putters

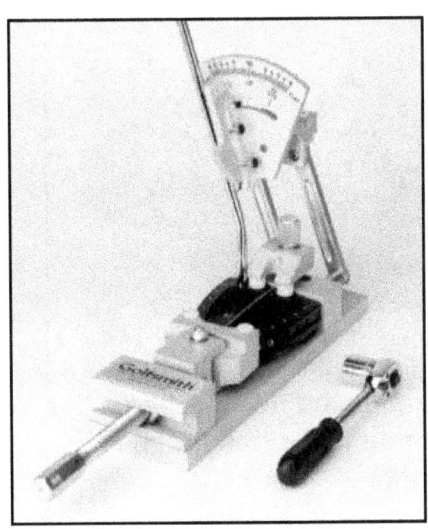

Adjusting putter lofts and lies has always been an enjoyable task for me. Unlike setting the specs on a set of irons you can execute the adjustment pretty quickly on a single putter. However the shorter time factor isn't the reason I enjoy bending putters so much. It really has more to do with the wide variety of design styles that must be navigated through. Aside from the different types of materials bending an iron or wood hosel are pretty straight forward. All take the same approach to in achieving the final bend spec. Putters are produced from many different types of metals in addition to having hosels or no hosels from which to work with. Sometimes it is a hosel that needs to be bent. For other models it can be the shaft. And like woods, there are occasions where the face angle needs to be straightened out. It is also a pleasure to see the benefits from your bending results almost immediately. Granted, a large volume of the putters I have adjusted were either in a tour van or in the workshop of business. In both cases putting greens were immediately accessible to observe the results of the adjustments.

A bench vise works well for securing a putter head that requires a lie angle change. Be sure to use vise pads to protect the putter's finish.

It doesn't take much equipment to pursue putter bending adjustments. In many cases a bending bar is not necessary, depending on the type of material that the hosel is made of. All that is necessary is a manner in which to secure the putter head during the bend. Something as simple as a bench vise can hold a putter in place for lie angle adjustments. Or you can invest in a premium putter bending unit that is accompanied with loft and lie gauges for measuring as the putter is being adjusted. I personally use a wide variety of tools for adjusting putter lofts and lies. There are many occasions where the simplest tool is also the best tool for the job.

Let's begin with some of the simple tools that are available. As previously mentioned a bench vice works well for adjusting lie angles. One can be purchased for very little money at a discount tool store like Harbor Freight or from one of the big box hardware stores such as Lowe's or Home Depot. With the vice mounted to a workbench it serves a multitude of custom club services that go beyond putter lie adjustments. While an small inexpensive vise can work well for putter adjustments it may be worth the investment to purchase a larger heavy duty vise that can be used for

Any economy putter vice can hold a head in place as the hosel is bent. Loft and lie must be measured using a separate tool.

everything from grip installations to securing other equipment used in club alterations.

To adjust the lie angle on a putter using a bench vise it is important to position the putter in a manner that is easiest for you to manipulate. I personally prefer orientating the toe of the putter downward in the grip of the vise. In this position the face is perpendicular to the ground. Any adjustment to the lie angle will be executed by bending the hosel upward to flatten it or downward to make the putter more upright.

Some club technicians may prefer to position the face downward instead. With the putter in this orientation a lie angle adjustment will be made by bending the hosel on a parallel plane to the ground.

Another inexpensive device for securing a putter head is an economy putter bending tool. There are two that I use with frequency. One is a bench mounted device that is a simple "U" shaped fixture with a vertically positioned screw clamp on the top of it. The putter is placed into the tool and the top clamp screws down onto the topline of the putter to hold it securely. Older versions of this same tool did not incorporate the top clamp and it still worked well but the putter head could shift around some within the fixture.

While an economy putter bender can be purchased from a tool supplier such as Golfsmith it is also possible for the industrious club technician to make a similar tool in one's shop. It can easily be produced out of wood using good quality hardware to keep the fixture from weakening.

A long time friend of mine, Guerin Rife, started his putter company back in the mid-1990's. He became an overnight sensation about ten years later with his 2-Bar and Hybrid putter designs being used by scores of touring professionals. Guerin created an inexpensive lie adjustment tool he used frequently at tour events.   The putter company tour representatives are positioned around the practice putting green during the practice rounds of the tournaments. If a tour pro was interested in trying out a new putter he would address one of the many reps and try out the wares. Often an adjustment was required to get the lie angle correct for the golfer. This would require the tour rep to leave the putting green and take the club to one of the many equipment trailers at the tournament site. Quite often while the tour rep was getting the putter adjusted for the pro another company's tour rep would approach the player and get one of their putters into his hands.

This type of activity doesn't bode well with tour reps so Guerin decided to create a bending fixture he could use right there on the practice green. He wasn't about to lose his player prospects to a competitor by leaving the practice green. The device he created is a simpler form of the economy putter bender. A sheet of heavy duty ABS plastic is folded into the shape of a "U" with a slot cut into one side of it. A putter is placed face first into the fixture and then the tool and putter are placed resting on the ground. At this point the technician places both feet on the tool and with hands grasping the putter's grip an upright or flatter bending force is applied to the putter's shaft.

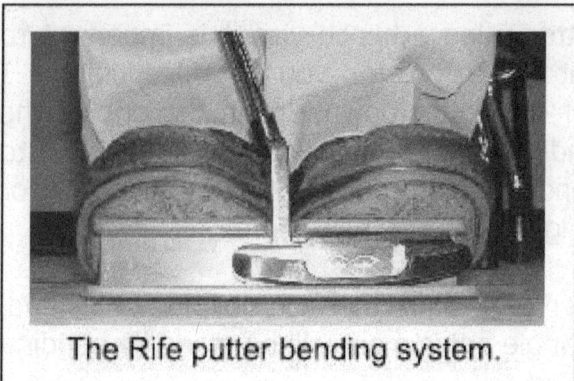
The Rife putter bending system.

The first time an individual observes this adjustment operation there is the feeling that a putter is going to end up in two pieces. This is an operation best suited for a shaft bend as opposed to a hosel bend, however I will expound on that a little further here in the book.

A serious club technician will likely invest in a premium putter bending machine. There are a couple of models I have used in the past and the most versatile turns out to be a moderately priced one. Retailing around $250 I was able to convince my toolmaker supplier to economize and improve and previous bending machine that sold for twice as much.

A premium bending unit must be designed to accommodate all putter sizes on the market. Over the past few years we have seen some overly large putter footprints launched into the marketplace. Mallet style putters have much larger footprints to them than blades and it is important to seek out a putter bending machine that handles both design styles.

Another necessary feature to a premium bender will be the loft and

A premium putter bending unit will secure the head during its adjustment in addition to reading the lie and loft measurements.

lie reading gauges. This makes adjusting and reading the results immediate without having to place the putter in an external loft/lie measurement unit. Adjustments and readings can be executed quickly by having the gauges as part of the machine.

There are some pretty high-end bending machines available on the market for club technicians to use. Scotty Cameron makes one of the most premium machines on the market however they are not accessible to everyone that wants one. Mitchell Golf has been manufacturing a premium putter bender for many years. It is CNC milled and designed to be quite accurate. I have had feedback from professional club technicians who have used each of the premium putter bending units mentioned here state that the Golfsmith model is by far the best value for the price.

Securing a putter head for bending is an important factor in successfully adjusting the loft and lie angles to the desired spec. A means to actually bend the putter is also a necessary tool. Sometimes it is as simple as using your hands while on other occasions a bending bar may be necessary.

Hands can be used to grasp the putter's shaft in order to bend it more upright or flatter for a no-hosel design. Unlike irons and woods which nearly all have hosels, there are many putter styles that do not have a hosel to them. When adjustments are made to these putters the shaft is being bent, not a hosel. For this execution a tool is not necessary. The force to bend the shaft only needs to be exerted through the technician's hands. We'll address this in further detail in the section that follows regarding the materials used in putter manufacturing.

This specialty bending bar grasps a small hosel opening while providing evenly distributed force along the putter shaft.

When a hosel needs to be adjusted a bending bar will usually be necessary to grasp the putter head and place the necessary force to the hosel. In most cases the same bending bar used for irons and woods can also be used for putters. However if your shop is like mine you have a wide assortment of bending bars from which to work with. There are knuckle styles

The Perfect Bend

and angles that work better in some situations than others. The same is true when it comes to putters.

There are also some putter-only style bending bars that have been developed. Some utilize a wider spread instead of a knuckle to manipulate the bend while others can grasp both the hosel and the shaft at the same time. This latter design is an excellent tool to have in your shop as it is one of the few that can also realign a crooked hosel back to a neutral orientation. Again, I'll address more of this bend in the bending execution section of this book.

Bending Different Putter Materials

Before jumping into hosel bending of putters we must first take a look at the design of the putter that needs to be adjusted. Does it have a hosel? If yes, then we must consider the type of material that the hosel is manufactured from.

We know there are primarily two different materials used in wood construction – titanium and stainless steel. Getting familiar with these two materials and their bending tendencies takes some getting used to. With irons we have softer materials that are either cast or forged and harder materials that are typically cast. Again, becoming familiar with the bending characteristics of these metals takes a little time adjusting them. Now we come to putters.

Putters that are investment cast are usually produced in 17-4, 431 or 304 stainless steel. If you recall from iron bending each of these materials have a different Thrust Rating and bending methodology. While a jerk force is recommended for 17-4 and 431 stainless steel irons we will be using a gradual force for putters produced in all three of these materials. The reason for this approach is that the hosel design is usually going to be much thinner on a putter than on an iron. With an iron we are attempting to bend the circular walls surrounding the golf shaft. A bend to a putter usually takes place below the shafted portion of the hosel. Instead it is a hosel post that is being bent, not the housing where the shaft is epoxied to the hosel.

Follow the same guidelines regarding the number of degrees the hosel can be bent for the appropriate material. This is the safest approach however with more experience at bending the different metals you will find that you can take certain hosel designs a degree or two farther when compared to iron adjustments. The thinner design of the hosel itself can provide a greater bending range in some models. Again, experience in bending many different types of materials and hosel configurations will lead to your expanded bending knowledge.

In addition to the three most popular stainless steels used in irons there are additional metals used in putter design. Carbon steel is very popular for both investment cast models and CNC milled designs. If the past is investment cast 8620 carbon steel will be the material that is used. For a 100% CNC milled putter a 1000 series carbon still or even a soft stainless steel (303 or 304) will be used in the design. Frequently a 100% CNC milled putter design begins as a roughly shaped forged part. Some 100% CNC milled putters start off as an oversized investment cast part that gets milled down to its final shape. And finally, the most premium of the 100% CNC milled putters are shaped from a square or rectangular block of steel. In each case a manufacturer may state that the putter is 100% CNC milled however there are differences in the initial block of material that is machined.

Regardless of the approach taken to arrive at a 100% CNC milled putter head in all cases the materials used will be either a soft carbon or soft stainless steel. Follow the same bending guidelines to adjust these hosel materials as you would with an iron adjustment. The biggest difference between bending the carbon steel hosels on a putter versus an iron is that the putter will usually not be chrome plated. Most carbon steel putters have the metal protected so it will not rust. For many years black oxide, also known as gun bluing, was applied to the surfaces of the carbon steel to prohibit rust. In more recent years a variety of surface protection has been used ranging from an assortment of different plating processes that can include dipping operations (black nickel, chrome plating, champagne plating) or vacuum applications (physical vapor deposition, ion plating). Learning the characteristics of each of the plating's ability to bend takes time and experience. For example, a nickel or chrome plating from one manufacturer may be more conducive to accepting a bend without wrinkling than those from another manufacturer. Each plating operation yields different results in the surface materials, yet the surfaces can look no different from one another. As a bend is being applied to the putter's hosel pay particular attention to how the adjustment affects the surface finish of the head. It is always best to advise the club owner that even though it is possible to adjust the head to the desired spec there could be surface imperfections that could result from the adjustment.

Another material commonly used in putters is aluminum. There are inexpensive aluminums that are cast and then the aerospace grade aluminums that are usually CNC milled. Look at the surface finish of the aluminum putter to determine if there are machining marks or not. If the putter appears to have been milled then it is likely a high grade aluminum alloy that has undergone a heat treatment. Limit the hosel bend to 2° for this material. You will often find that aluminum headed putters either use a no-hosel design or will sometimes incorporate a hosel made of a steel material for increased durability. The challenge using aluminum in a putter design is that most aluminum hosels are the weak link in the design change. Many golfers will lean on their putters as they wait their turn to putt. A moderate amount of force is enough to break an aluminum hosel so most putter designers avoid using aluminum in the hosel.

If there are no milling marks anywhere on the aluminum putter head the design likely has been cast. No more than 1° of adjustment should be made to the hosel if the putter has one. Again, most designers know the durability limitations of using aluminum in the hosel.

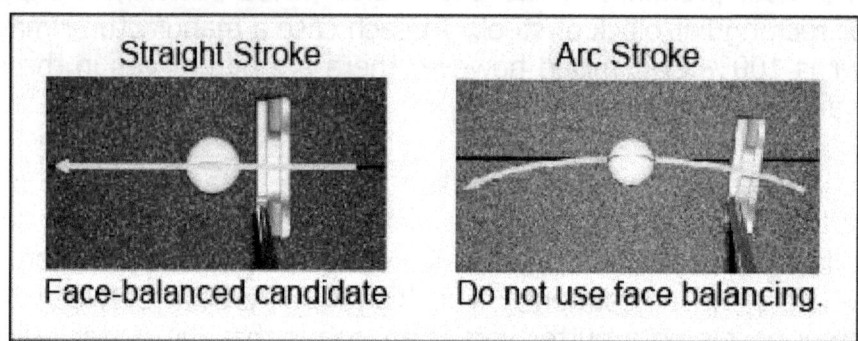

One putter design that has purposely used an aluminum hosel is the Rife 2-Bar putter. In fact, when purchasing one of these models the buyer automatically receives one of the ABS plastic putter adjustment tools to set the lie angle properly. A specially heat treated aluminum hosel post has been used in the design so that the lie angle can be adjusted to the proper fit. This aerospace grade aluminum can be safely adjusted 5°.

Brass has been a material used in putter design for many decades. Many golfers today still play with a Bulls Eye brass putter which has gone through more minor design iterations than most any other putter on the market. The brass is very pliable and bends effortlessly. Brass can be bent 15° without any durability issues.

Cause and Effect Adjusting Putter Loft & Lie Angles

There are many specifications involving golf equipment that have an influence on another important spec when it has been adjusted. When it comes to putters there are two very important specs that attention must be paid to because of the domino effect on others. The first of these are lie angles and their effect on face balancing.

A face balanced putter has a very stable plane to the striking surface of the putter. It is designed to stay square to the target line throughout the putting stroke. For a golfer who keeps the face square during the takeaway and follow through of the putter a face balanced design is good for helping to retain a square face angle. The golfer that fans the face open on the takeaway or has a putting plane shaped more like an arc should not use a face balanced putter. The design of the face balancing actually inhibits the natural putting stroke of the golfer who rolls the face open and closed throughout the putting stroke.

A putter that is face balanced has the axis of the shaft intersect the center of the putter's face. This can be achieved through the design of the hosel, by centering the shaft to the face or through a multi-bend shaft configuration. Most any putter head design can be made face balanced by reconstructing the shaft axis to run through the face. Some golfers and technicians believe that a non-face balanced putter can be converted to one using weight distribution. This is not feasibly possible. Face balancing is created through geometry, not mass distribution.

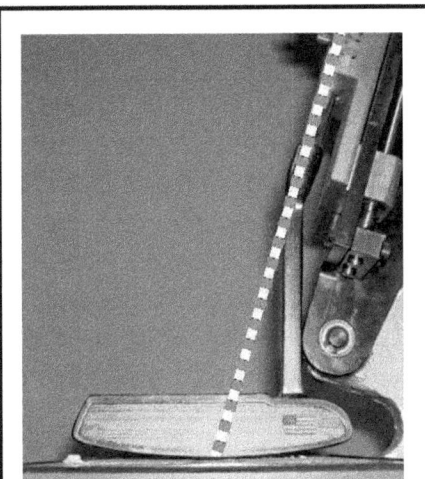

Face balancing is achieved by orientating the axis of the shaft with the center of the putter face.

It is easy to identify a face balanced putter from a non-face balanced model. Rest the putter shaft on a table with the head extended over the edge. What direction does the toe of the putter face with the club at rest? If the heel and toe are on the same plane the face of the putter will be pointing directly upward. It will be parallel to the ground and table top. A putter that rests in this orientation is a face balanced putter.

If the toe of the putter drops down so that the face is slanted towards the ground the putter is not face balanced. Likewise, a toe that points skyward is not a face balanced putter either.

It is important to pay close attention to the adjustment to lie angles on face balanced putters. Adjusting the lie angle too upright or flat will take the shaft axis off of its intersection with the center of the face and tilt it either more heel-ward (for an upright adjustment) or toe-ward (for a flatter adjustment). Going too far upright or flat on the lie angle bend will take the putter completely out of face balancing. This may or may not be important to the golfer who is going to use it.

 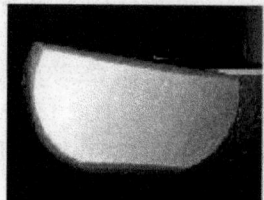 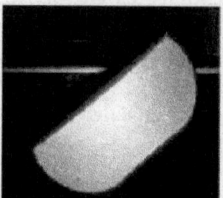

Face Balanced - Face is parallel to ground.   Lie angle bent too flat raises to upward.   Lie angle bent too upright makes toe drop down.

It is acceptable to alter a face balanced putter's lie angle a few degrees that there is only a small impact on the face balancing. Notice the photo on the following page. This is the same putter and its face orientation after numerous lie adjustments. You can see the effects of bending upright and flatter. The left photo has had the lie angle adjusted 2° upright from its original lie angle. The toe drops ever so slightly but is parallel enough to be considered a face balance putter. A greater lie adjustment change will result in a non-face balanced result like the center and right putters.

The other spec that is very important to pay attention to is the loft adjustment. As with adjusting iron lofts, there is a direct impact on the bounce angle of the putter's sole when its loft is adjusted. Most putters are designed with a neutral bounce angle. Altering the sole so that it has a bounce angle to it will make the face of the putter roll closed when placed on a firm surface. If loft is reduced so is the sole's bounce angle. A putter with a negative bounce angle will roll into an open position on a firm surface. To many golfers a putter face that rolls open or closed is not desirable. The putter should set up square to the target line when it is at rest. Careful consideration must be taken into account when adjusting the loft on putters. A small amount of loft adjustment (1°) is preferred over something greater due to the bounce angle affects.

Putter Rolls Open - It has negative bounce (too much loft removed).   Putter Rolls Closed - Too much bounce (from loft being added).   Putter sets square as expected. Sole rests flush to the ground.

If the golfer desires for more loft to be added or reduced to the putter it may be necessary for the club technician to grind the putter sole so that it results in a neutral bounce. Do not pursue this activity unless you are familiar with custom grinding.

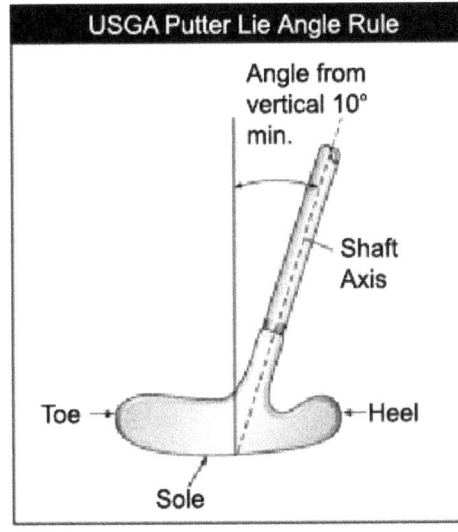

While it is important to pay attention to adjustments and their effects on other specifications there are another series of concerns that must be kept in mind – the USGA's Rules of Golf. The United States Golf Association establishes not only the rules by which to play the game of golf but also equipment standards. Within those standards are limitations on some of the equipment specifications. When it comes to putters there are rules that govern the degree to which the loft and lie may be adjusted.

Looking at the lie angle first the USGA has a limit to how upright a lie angle may be but no rule regarding how flat it can be. In their rule the USGA has tried to disallow a completely vertical upright lie angle. The putter's lie angle must be at least 10° flat from a vertical position. The way most club technicians would look at this rule is that the lie angle cannot be any more upright than 80°. When Sam Snead was having putting woes and transitioned to a side saddle style of putting it required that the putter have a vertical lie angle. This was observed as a non-traditional putting style and the ruling was intended to dissuade the unique putting setup.

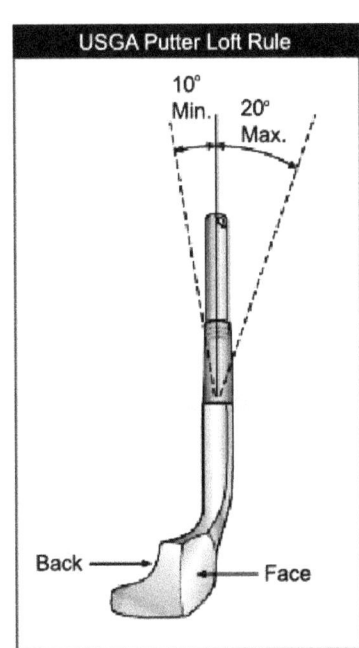

While the 10° minimum rule prevents golfers from putting in this non-traditional manner an extremely unorthodox putting style could be developed with an extremely flat putter too. There are no rules in preventing this however the advantages appear to lean towards a very upright putter versus a very flat putter when it comes to getting the ball into the hole.

There is also a rule governing the amount of loft on a putter. Twenty degrees is the maximum and minus-10° is the minimum. It is documented that around 3°-4° is he optimum launch angle of the ball on an efficient putt. With that amount of launch the backspin to the ball is minimized and the skid zone, where the ball is the least stable, is shortened. So why would a golfer elect for as much as 20° or -10° on their putter? These limitations have been established for a reason. The USGA is exposed to a number of unique clubs with non-traditional applications on an ongoing basis.

One example of such a club is a putter designed to hold a forward press. Once a golfer forward presses the putter it is de-lofted. There are varying degrees of a forward press and some are more severe than others. I once placed 14° of loft on one of Arnold Palmer's putters so he could experiment holding a forward press during his putting stroke. Fortunately he was using a brass Bulls Eye putter which easily accommodated the adjustment. Thirty minutes after making the bend, Royce his caddy was back asking me to adjust it back to its original loft.

The putter loft rule places limitations on some golfers' creative approach to the putting stroke. I believe another purpose of the rule is to help categorize exactly what a putter is. For example, chippers are popular club designs with many golfers. They incorporate more loft than a putter; usually loft similar to a short or mid iron. However the length of chippers are very similar to putters since they are used only around the putting green. The maximum of 20° of loft rule will clearly limit to what the chipper's design characteristics can be. Producing a chipper with more than 20° of loft requires that it be designed under the same guidelines as an iron. Most chippers are in fact designed using these guidelines.

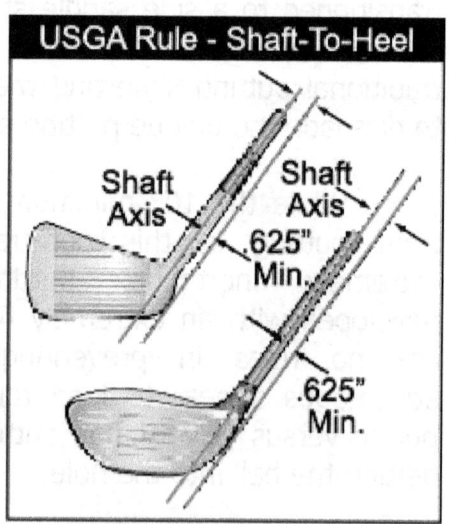

However by designing a chipper with less than 20° of loft there are numerous short game elements that can now be included in the club. This is where putter guidelines preside. For example, only putters are allowed to be face balanced. All other clubs must have the hosel axis with 0.625" of the heel of the clubhead. If you recall, face balancing can only be achieved by aligning the shaft axis with the center of the clubface. By keeping the loft below 20° a chipper can be categorized as a putter and be eligible to have a face balanced hosel design.

A flat faced grip can only be used on putters. Since putters can be designed at standard, mid and over-length specs it is the loft rule that governs the use of the flat sided style putting grip. The loft rule also governs the groove design limitations. Grooves used on a putter face are independent from those used on irons and woods.

It is important to be aware of these equipment rules when working on the adjustment of golf equipment. Knowing the limitations you have as a club technician on the loft and lie angles for putters keeps you from taking a USGA conforming club and turning it into a non-conforming putter.

The Execution — Adjusting Putter Loft & Lie Angles

Making adjustments to a putter's loft and lie angle are very straight forward. As discussed in the material section that precedes this it is important to examine the type of hosel design on the putter. There are three typical hosel designs used. With each of these three designs a different bending approach is used. Remember, the type of material the hosel is constructed from is an integral part of executing the adjustment. Keep that in mind as the application of the appropriate bend process is executed. The three different hosel configurations are:

- Hosel stem
- Post (or shank)
- No-Hosel

Hosel Stem

Putters designed with a hosel stem are the most common style sold. The stem itself is only a portion of the hosel. Its most upper element is the receptor where the shaft is bonded to the putter head. The adjustment to the hosel will take place on the stem portion, not the shaft receptor. You will find putters designed with hosel stems will have either a female or male shaft receptor. The female shaft receptor is one where the shaft tip is inserted into the hosel opening. The male version is a post, or shank, that extends from the top of the hosel. With this design the shaft tip is installed over the male hosel post. Epoxy is applied to the out circumference of the shaft for

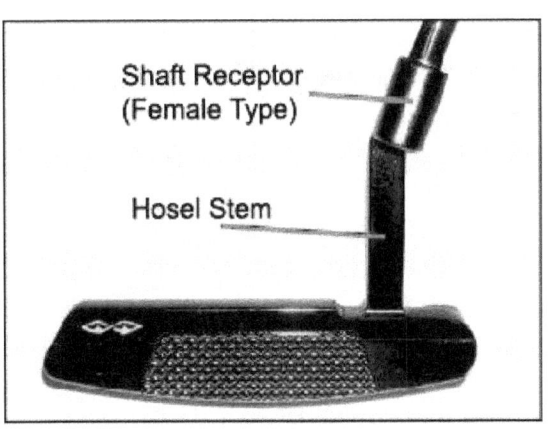

the female hosel installation and it is applied to the inner diameter of the shaft for the male hosel post.

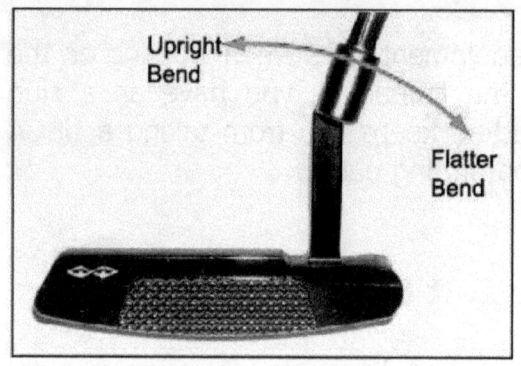

The type of shaft receptor is not important when it comes to adjusting the loft or lie of the hosel stem. The location of the bending force will be applied to the stem, not the receptor.

To adjust the lie angle of the putter the bending direction will be either towards to putter's toe or heel. A bending force towards the toe will make the lie angle more upright. It is important to keep the bend plane parallel to the face of the putter otherwise the loft may also be affected during the adjustment.

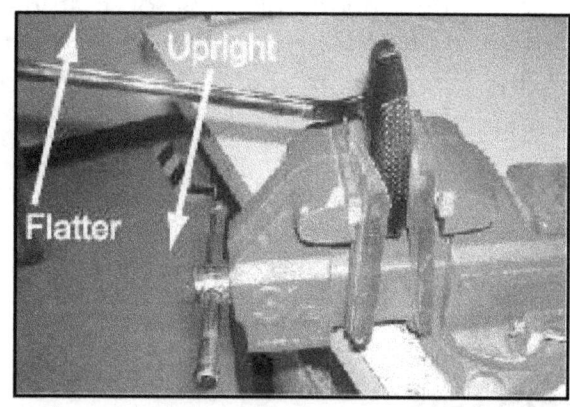

A force bending towards the heel side of the putter will flatten the lie angle. As with the upright bend keep the bend on a plane parallel to the face so that only the lie angle is affected.

To execute the lie angle bend you will be using either your hands or a bending bar. When working with soft materials such as carbon steel or a soft series of stainless steel (usually 303 or 304) I like to begin the bend using only my hands. With most hosel stem designs the soft material gives in to the bending force applied by hand. Executing the hand-only bend should take place approximately 12" above the hosel receptor on the golf shaft. If additional force is necessary shifting the hands to a higher grasping point on the shaft will help to exert more force on the hosel.

Hosel stem style putters manufactured from harder materials will require a bending bar to adjust the lie. The bending bar should be oriented in a direction away from the heel of the putter. If the putter is secured in a playing position a force towards the toe will take the lie angle more upright and a bend towards the ground will flatten the lie.

If the putter is secured into a bench vise the toe will likely be pointing down towards the ground. Position the bending bar upright away from the toe. Pulling the bar towards the ground will make the putter more upright and forcing it towards the ceiling will flatten it.

For the club technician that secures the putter in a bench vise with the face positioned upwards the bending bar will need to be pointing away from the heel parallel to the ground. A bending force away from the putter will flatten its lie angle while a force in the opposite direction will make the lie angle more upright.

Adjusting the loft on hosel stem style models positions the bending bar forces on a 90° orientation to the lie angle adjustments. To begin with, determine if the head material is soft enough to adjust by hand. If it is the hands will be positioned within the first 12" of the shaft tip. This is where the applied force will take place to either increase or decrease the loft. If the material is a harder steel then a bending bar will be necessary. The knuckle of the bending bar will be placed around the hosel stem and the bar will be positioned either forward towards the target line (perpendicular to the face) or rearward (180° the opposite direction).

Test the adjustment by hand first. If the metal is soft enough the hosel stem will bend. Use a bending bar if the putter is made of a harder steel.

With the bending bar positioned forward of the face a downward force will add more loft to the putter. If using your bare hands to execute the bend to a soft metal hosel then a forward bend to the shaft will increase the putter's loft.

To reduce the loft the bending bar will require an upwards force on the hosel stem. Bare hand bending will require a rearward force to the shaft in order to decrease the loft.

As with iron and wood adjustments the technician must develop a feel to determine the amount of loft being adjusted on any given bending force. With more experience a technician will be able to execute the correct amount of force with each subsequent adjustment to putters.

While loft and lie angles are a primary focus when it comes to hosel stem adjustments there is one other specification that sometimes needs to be addressed with these types of hosels – face angle. From a design standpoint every putter should have a square face angle as its specification. Unfortunately the face angle can be altered due to manufacturing issues from the casting

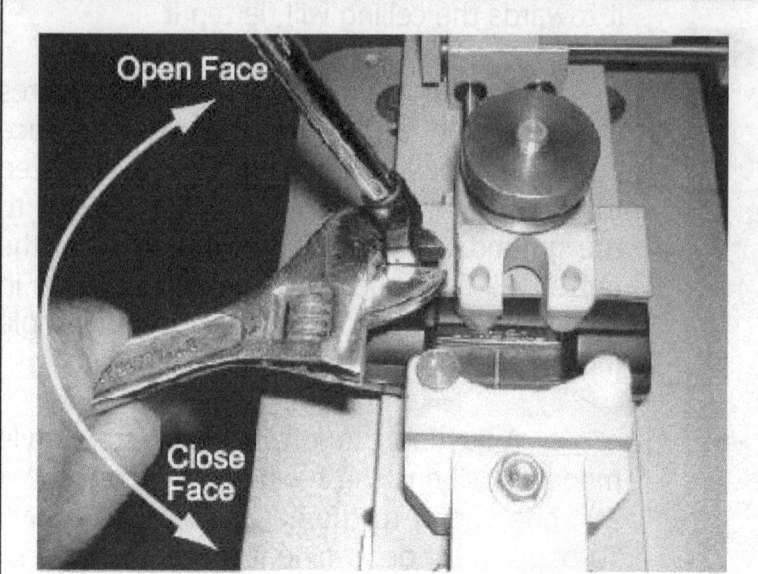

Use an adjustable wrench to straighten the face angle of a bent hosel stem. Sometimes two wrenches are required for harder steel hosels.

process, shock to a putter when it was dropped or as a result from a hosel bend. To a trained eye the putter just doesn't set up correctly and this is often the result of the hosel stem being twisted.

I have seen bad putter designs in the past where all of the hosel stems are twists and even though the correct loft and lie angles can be achieved there is a curvature to the hosel stem that was not intended to be part of the design. These turn out to be some of the most challenging adjustments to make.

It is important to secure the putter head in a bending machine. Trying to correct the hosel alignment with the putter locked into a bench vise or economy bending tool will lead to undesired twisting during the adjustment operation.

Historically I have used adjustable open end wrenches to try and correct the alignment of the hosel stem. Clamping two wrenches in opposite directions of one another provides the technician some maneuverability with the hosel orientation. This adjustment is all about getting the look of the putter right. Specifications are the secondary fix to this otherwise perplexing look.

A special putter bending tool has been developed to execute this same type of adjustment. The challenge of this adjustment is to sometimes isolate the bend of the hosel in a very restrictive location. For example, the very bottom of the hosel stem may need to be twisted more open while the most upper portion near the shaft receptor needs to be rotated closed. Such an adjustment cannot be done using a single bend.

In some cases a normal bending bar can be used in aligning the face angle correctly however a more specialized tool like the putter bending bar or other shop tools may be required to get the job done. It is up to the creativity of the equipment technician to achieve desirable results for some of these jobs.

Post (or Shank) Style Hosels

A putter with a post or shank hosel provides the technician very little real estate to grasp the hosel for bending purposes. When working with a hosel post there is very little material to the hosel itself. The male shank extends above the base of the body and the shaft is bonded over the post. Making an adjustment to this type of hosel will require some speculation on the part of the club technician.

Some hosel post designs may appear to be a no-hosel design because the shaft installs over the shank. Learn which models use a post design in order to adjust them appropriately.

The adjustment to the loft and lie can be made to the hosel post itself or to the shaft in the area directly above it. What must first be determined is the type of material that the head is constructed from. If it is steel then the preference would be to execute the bend at the very base of the shaft where it is positioned over the shank. The bend will be to the shank itself even though the bending bar will be positioned over the shaft tip.

If the putter is constructed from aluminum it may be best to avoid bending the hosel post (except in the case of the Rife putters). Most aluminum shanks will not accommodate a bend without snapping off. For these models the loft and lie adjustments must be made to the shaft above the shank.

If the male hosel post is to be bent then a bending bar is going to be required to execute the adjustment. Position the bending bar in the positions used to alter loft and lie on an iron or hosel stem style putter. The lie is adjusted by positioning the bending bar outwards away from the heel of the head. Adjust the lie keeping the bending bar on a parallel plane to the face.

A loft adjustment is made by extending the bar either forward towards the target line (perpendicular to the face) or rearward of the target line. The same forces will be applied to the bar to increase or reduce loft as on the hosel stem style putters.

There are two reasons why a technician would bend the shaft instead of the hosel shank on these styles of putters. The first has already been discussed in the fact that the material of the post may not be durable enough to accept an adjustment. The other is that the post may be so short that it is difficult to get the bending bar knuckle over it for an adjustment. In both of these cases a hand bend should take place on the shaft.

Grasp the shaft approximately 24"-30" above the shaft tip. Forcing the shaft on plain with the face either a force towards the toe (more upright) or towards the heel (flatter) will provide the appropriate lie angle adjustment. There will be a much greater amount of force used to make this adjustment than what was used via the hand method on the hosel stem design.

When adjusting the loft or lie by hand on the hosel stem design even though the hands were positioned on the shaft the bend occurred down in the hosel stem (because of its soft material). The shaft itself was only a lever. With a hand bend to a male hosel post design there is very little hosel so the bend will be occurring in the shaft, not the head. This is the purpose for placing the hands higher up the shaft. The area below the hands will be giving into the bending force.

The "Big Bend" Grabbing the grip and pulling the shaft in the direction of the bend. 15°- 45° bend is required to adjust a few degrees.

A much greater amount of force will be used to execute the adjustment. I call this particular angle adjustment using the shaft as the "big bend." All quality steel putter shafts are tempered and can accept such a bend. In order to execute a 2° bend the putter shaft will need to be forced anywhere from 15°- 45°. That is a mighty big bend for only a 2° adjustment. Bending using this method is a little scary to the novice. The fear is that the shaft will buckle or crease at some weak point along its axis. I have only run across non-tempered shafts during prototype testing from some inexpensive suppliers and in some discount store products. Name brand steel shafts such as True Temper, Rifle, FST and Nippon will have been tempered and can accept the "big bend" adjustments.

Early in my clubfitting career I found myself using a propane torch to adjust loft and lie angles using the putter shaft. Getting the shaft red hot allowed for a very precise alteration to it. With the shaft cooled down the scorched area would get re-polished back to a mirror finish and no one was the wise on how the bend was executed. However the propane process is not necessary. The big bend approach is much quick, doesn't require heat and prevents you from having to re-finish the shaft's cosmetics once the adjustment is done.

No-Hosel Putters

Many putters incorporate no hosel in their designs. The tip of the shaft protrudes directly into the putter head. Sometimes there may be a question on whether a putter is a no-hosel design or if there is a post extended from the head into the shaft. To be on the safe side many technicians approach any style in question as if it were a no-hosel putter.

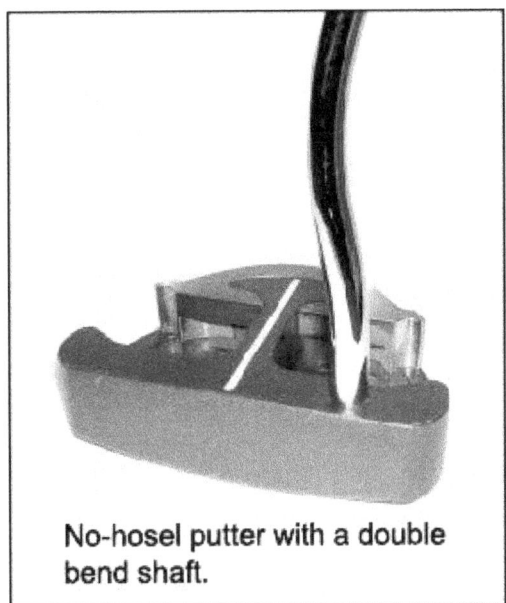

No-hosel putter with a double bend shaft.

There are two shaft styles used in no-hosel putters. As with hosel stem designs a straight shaft is used. Typically the shaft will be installed in the horizontal center of the putter face. This style of putter is usually referred to as a center shafted putter.

The other shaft style is a multi-bend design. Most common are double bend putter shafts however there are also single and triple bend designs used. The number of bends is irrelevant to the club technician for adjustment purposes. A no-hosel putter is going to utilize the big bend method of adjusting the loft and lie angle. All of the bending occurs on the shaft because there is no hosel to bend on the head.

The multi-bend putter shafts are designed under a USGA rule that states a putter cannot have a bend occurring 5" linearly from the ground line. Therefore it is important to keep any bend to a putter shaft below this 5" point. This is applicable to not only multi-bend putter shafts but also to straight putter shafts. The big bend method is going to be applied to adjusting the loft and lie of the putter.

With the big bend method no bending bar will be used - only the technician's hands. In fact, if a bending bar is used to try and adjust the loft or lie of a no-hosel putter shaft there is a strong likelihood that the knuckle of the bending bar will place a crease in the shaft at its contact point. The knuckle creates an area of stress on the shaft whereas the hand executed big bend displaces stress along the entire length of the shaft during its adjustment.

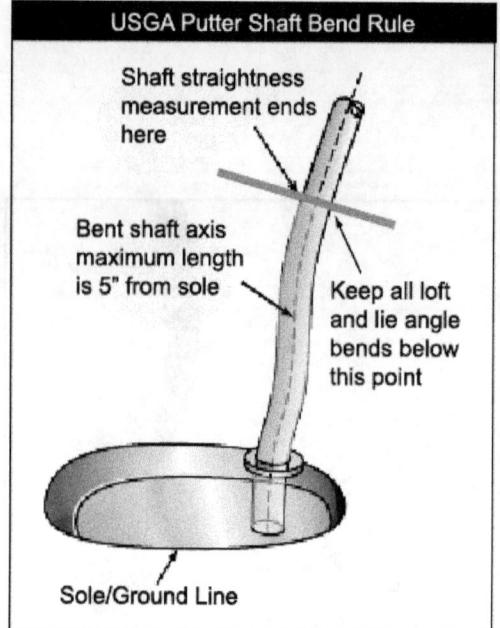

Forcing the shaft bend on a heel-to-toe plane, parallel with the face, will allow for the lie angle to be adjusted either more upright or flatter. This is no different than the adjustments made to the hosel stem or post style putters. Likewise, adjusting the loft of the putter will require a bending forced either forward of the face (to add loft) or rearward behind the putter (to remove loft). Keep in mind the effect that loft has on the bounce angle of the putter's sole. Concessions may have to be made to accommodate the loft adjustments due to the sole angle. Either the putter will need to have less loft adjusted or grinding to the sole's bounce angle may be necessary to keep the putter from rolling open or closed when it should be squared up.

Summarizing Putter Loft & Lie Adjustments

Due to the wide variety of putter hosel designs there are a number of different approaches to take in adjusting the loft and lie. Compared with irons and woods the execution of the adjustment is physically much easier. It may be a little more complex in understanding the correct approach however logic will often prevail. Looking at a putter's design and understanding is material composition are the two primary focal points in determining what type of hosel or shaft adjustment to make.

A well prepared equipment technician will have a variety of ways to fixture a putter head for loft and lie adjustments. In addition, there may be benefits in having a varied selection of bending bars available for grasping the hosel.

When in doubt always begin the adjustment procedure using only your hands to execute the bend. With experience the technician will learn which brands and models utilize harder steels versus softer materials. As with adjusting irons there is always a higher confidence when applying a bend to a softer metal.

The exercise of bending and breaking numerous styles of iron hosels may not be the most economical when it comes to getting acquainted with putters. I have only broken two putter hosels over the course of my career. In both cases they were models that had been die cast out of zinc and I was not aware of their material construction. Both putters were being marketed as a premium design however neither got far from the launching pad. Quality and being able to work on the equipment go hand in hand.

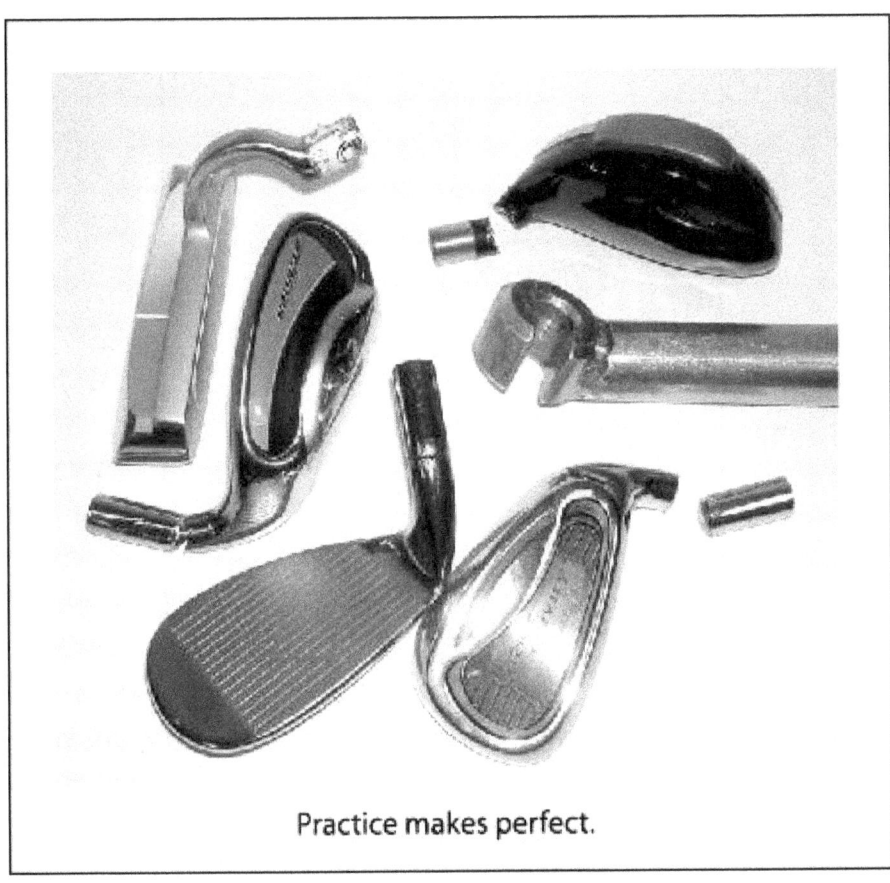

Practice makes perfect.

If you found *The Perfect Bend* to be an informative golf equipment manual then you will likely also benefit from the golf fitting guidance Jeff Sheets teaches in *The Perfect Fit*. This 270 page book covers every aspect of the golf club fitting process. Beginning with the flight laws and their cause & effect is the first stepping stone to a successful clubfitting. The components of the club are reviewed along with the fitting protocols for drivers, fairway and hybrid woods, irons, wedges, putters and golf balls. From the tried and true fitting process of decades past to using launch monitors, moment of inertia scales and optimized balance weighting, *The Perfect Fit* is the guide to fitting today's golfer equipment to today's golfer.

Available at www.theperfectfitbook.com.

www.ingramcontent.com/pod-product-compliance
Lightning Source LLC
LaVergne TN
LVHW061343060426
835512LV00016B/2648